KINGS
QUEENS
KNIGHTS
& JESTERS

Making
Medieval Costumes

KINGS
QUEENS
KNIGHTS
& JESTERS

Making
Medieval Costumes

By
LYNN EDELMAN
SCHNURNBERGER

In Association with The Metropolitan Museum of Art

drawings by Alan Robert Showe
photographs by Barbara Brooks and Pamela Hort

HARPER & ROW, PUBLISHERS
New York, Hagerstown, San Francisco, London

Kings, Queens, Knights and Jesters
Making Medieval Costumes
Copyright © 1978 by Lynn Edelman Schnurnberger and
The Metropolitan Museum of Art
All rights reserved. No part of this book may be used or
reproduced in any manner whatsoever without written
permission except in the case of brief quotations embodied
in critical articles and reviews. Printed in the United
States of America. For information address Harper & Row,
Publishers, Inc., 10 East 53rd Street, New York, N.Y. 10022.
Published simultaneously in Canada by Fitzhenry & Whiteside
Limited, Toronto.
FIRST EDITION

Library of Congress Cataloging in Publication Data
Schnurnberger, Lynn Edelman.
    Kings, queens, knights, and jesters.

    SUMMARY: Instructions for making medieval costumes such
as king, monk, knight, peasant, and minstrel, with facts
about the medieval period.
    1. Costume—Juvenile literature. 2. Costumes—History
—Medieval, 500-1500—Juvenile literature. [1. Costume.
2. Costume—History—Medieval, 500-1500. 3. Civilization,
Medieval] I. Showe, Alan Robert. II. Brooks,
Barbara. III. Hort, Pamela. IV. New York (City).
Metropolitan Museum of Art. V. Title. VI. Title:
Medieval costumes.
TT633.S3   646.4'7   77-25682
ISBN 0-06-025241-3
ISBN 0-06-025242-1 lib. bdg.

To Howie, who believes everything is possible,
and through his guidance, love and confidence in me
helps it to happen.

ACKNOWLEDGMENTS

The opportunity of working with both The Metropolitan Museum of Art and Harper & Row on this manuscript brought me together with many talented people whose advice and expertise helped to make this book a reality.

My thanks to Robie Rogge of The Metropolitan Museum of Art, whose eye for detail and aim for perfection set high standards for the production of this book, and whose enthusiasm and day-to-day involvement afforded me continuity and support; to Timothy B. Husband, Assistant Curator in Charge of Administration at The Cloisters, for his encouragement of this project; to Nancy Kueffner, Associate Museum Educator at The Cloisters, who oversees the entire Medieval Festival and has fostered the growth of this and other costume projects at the museum; to Elizabeth Glass of the Metropolitan, who searched for photographs to accompany the text and meticulously catalogued those selected.

Thanks to my editor at Harper & Row, Elizabeth Gordon, who enthusiastically accepted this project and edited the manuscript with precision; to Kohar Alexanian, who designed the book, for her patience and ability to include the wealth of photographs and illustrations we wanted to accompany the text; to Joanne Ryder, who reviewed the craft instructions; and to Renée Cafiero, who copyedited the manuscript, for her helpful suggestions in making the instructions in this book as clear as possible.

My thanks to Simone Colina and Robert Koch, who posed for many of the how-to photographs; to my family and friends for their interest and encouragement; and a final, very special thanks to the "journeymen" and "apprentices" who are pictured in this book. These are the volunteers and elementary school students who participate in the workshops each summer; for all they have taught me and allowed me to teach them, for the energy, ability and curiosity they lend to the workshops and the Festival each summer.

The Cloisters Medieval Festival project was supported by grants from the National Endowment for the Arts in Washington, D.C., a Federal agency, and The Metropolitan Museum of Art.

✣ CONTENTS

Introduction   x

Three Basic Patterns:
The Circle, The T, The Tunic   1

Medieval Characters   21

Decorating Your Costume   53

Accessories for Your Costume   72

Uses for Medieval Costumes   112

✤INTRODUCTION

Knights on horseback, ladies in long flowing gowns; a sorcerer stirring up his cauldron, a court jester in floppy hat and bells; King Arthur at the Round Table, Robin Hood and his men in Sherwood Forest. These are some of the people who lived in the Middle Ages. You know some of their names, and may have pictures in your mind of what they looked like. This book will tell you more about their lives and how they dressed, and it will tell you how to make the costumes that they wore.

The Middle Ages began to take shape in Europe from around A.D. 350 to A.D. 800 and lasted until the Renaissance, about A.D. 1550 (the Renaissance started somewhat earlier in Italy). For most of this time, everybody wore a variation of the same costume. Women, men and children alike all wore loose-fitting gowns that were shaped like T's and over these gowns they wore either CIRCLE-shaped capes or TUNICs for added warmth and protection. But everybody didn't look the same. The knight and the peasant both wore tunics, but the peasant's tunic was made out of wool, while the knight's was made out of loops of steel called "chain mail" so he would be protected in battle. All clothes were handmade, but the noble had a dressmaker to create his outfits, while the peasant sewed his own clothes. The peasant worked for the noble, and in exchange for his work the peasant received food, protection, a place to live and cloth to make his clothing. The noble provided the peasant with drab, inexpensive wools, but for his own clothes the noble imported linen from Reims in France and silks from the Far East. The noblewoman's gown was made out of the finest textiles, decorated with gold threads and trimmed with fur, while the peasant wore a simple unadorned dress of coarse wool. It wasn't the shape of medieval clothing that made the nobles' costumes different from the peasants'; it was the material their clothing was made from.

The costumes described in this book were worn from the time of Charlemagne (A.D. 800) until the middle of the fourteenth century. Because all of the costumes are a combination of just three shapes, it is easy to make medieval costumes. In the first chapter you will find instructions for making the T, the TUNIC and the CIRCLE. Next you will find descriptions of the people who lived in the Middle Ages and how they dressed. Decide what character you want to be and cut out the shapes you need for your costume. Then read about how to decorate your costume and what accessories to add.

This book will serve as a source of instructions and ideas for making medieval costumes. You will be offered many choices. After all, you and your friends may dress similarly, but you don't dress exactly alike. So, too, noblemen or knights dressed in a certain manner, but they were not carbon copies of each other. Pick and choose from the patterns and suggestions offered, add ideas of your own and you will be able to create a unique and personal medieval costume.

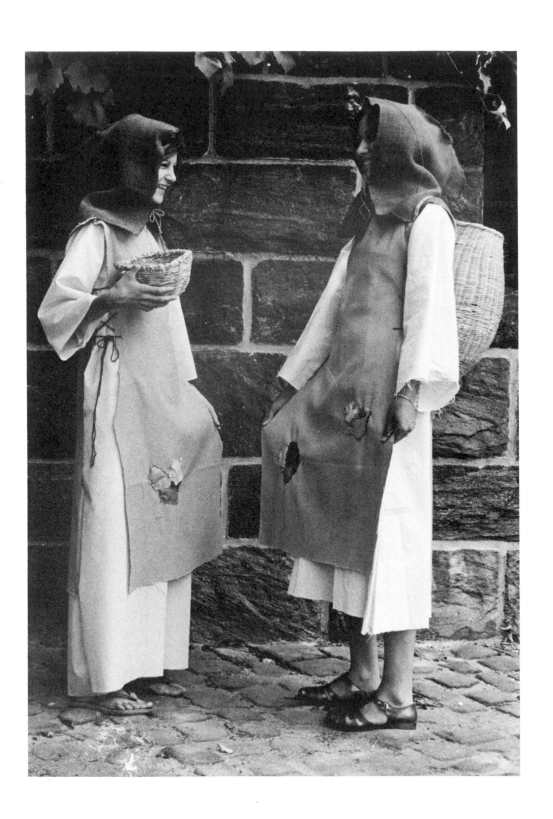

THREE BASIC PATTERNS:

❖THREE BASIC PATTERNS:
The CIRCLE, The T,
The TUNIC

HOW TO CHOOSE MATERIAL
FOR YOUR COSTUME

While it would be authentic to use linen, silk, chain mail and other "real" medieval materials, these are very expensive. You can often make a more imaginative costume by improvising with other materials.

Felt is the easiest fabric to work with, because the edges won't unravel when you cut out your costume shape. If you use cotton, polyester, burlap, velvet or almost any other fabric, you will have to do some extra sewing and hem the edges of the costume. Give some consideration to where you will be wearing the costume; if it's to be worn in a summer pageant you won't want to use wool or velvet because you will be hot and uncomfortable. Make sure that the fabric you choose is large enough for the costume you want to make.

The simplest material will often produce the best costume. If you start with a plain piece of fabric you can make up your own design and choose your favorite colors to fill it in. The chapter "How to Decorate Your Costume" will describe medieval fabric designs and decorations and tell you how to apply them to your costume; you will be able to transform even the plainest piece of material into a richly embroidered- or brocaded-looking costume.

The Queen of Sheba. Detail from a tapestry, King Solomon and the Queen of Sheba *German, 15th century.*

1 How to Make the Circle

By using a circle for a pattern, you can make a costume out of one piece of material. All you have to do is cut an opening for your head in the middle of the circle and you have a cape, instantly—without any sewing. The cape was called a "cope" when worn by a member of the clergy, and a "cloak" or a "mantle" when worn by a nobleman. The first cape was probably worn by the caveman who wrapped a blanket around himself to keep warm. But it was in the Middle Ages, when capes were made from velvet, lined with fur and fastened with jeweled brooches, that the cape became an elegant coat.

WHAT SIZE PIECE OF MATERIAL WILL YOU NEED?

Since you will be making the back and the front of your costume at the same time, your circle will have to be fairly large. Sheets, bedspreads and old curtains are good for this project.

Length: Have someone measure you. Start at your shoulder and measure down to the point where you want the costume to end. This is the LENGTH OF YOUR COSTUME. Multiply this number by 2 to determine the length your piece of material should be.

Width: The width must be the same as the LENGTH. So your piece of material should be square.

Besides the material, you will need a tape measure, a pencil and scissors.

1. Lay out your square piece of material.
2. Fold it in half from top to bottom,
3. and in half again from left to right. The fold in the material should be on your left.

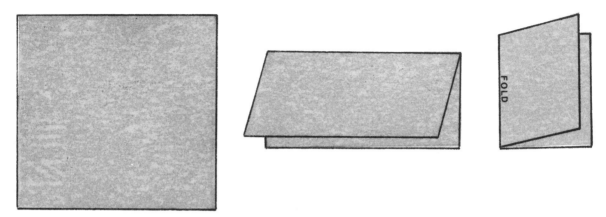

Now you want to make an arc which will connect the lower left-hand corner of the square to the upper right-hand corner:

4. Lay your tape measure diagonally across the folded material, with the zero at A.
5. Use a pencil and mark off the LENGTH OF YOUR COSTUME along this diagonal.

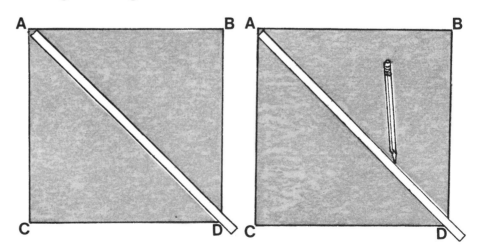

6. Keeping the zero at A, measure and mark off the LENGTH OF YOUR COSTUME in several places.
7. To make the arc, connect these points with a light pencil line. It should be a curve.
8. Carefully cut through all four layers of cloth along this line.

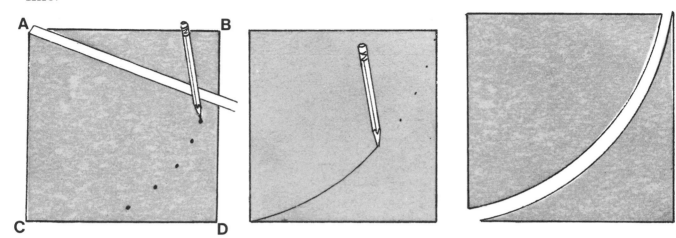

TO CUT AN OPENING FOR YOUR HEAD

Cut out a circle in the middle of the circle as an opening for your head:
9. Leave your material folded.
10. Place your tape measure with the zero at A again. Measure and mark off a length of 3 inches in several places.

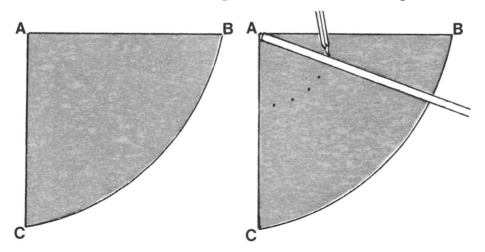

11. Connect these points with a light pencil line, also in a curve.

12. Cut along this line. Now unfold your material.

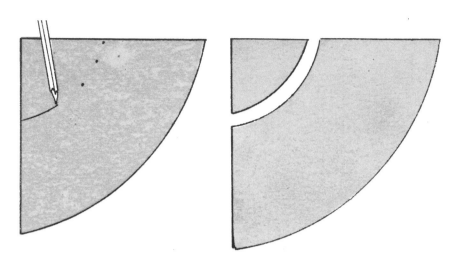

To Make A Semicircle

Sometimes you want to make a CIRCLE costume but you don't have a piece of material which is large enough. In this case you can make two half circles or SEMICIRCLES, which you will sew together. Remember to cut an opening for your head before you join these two pieces.

WHAT SIZE PIECE OF MATERIAL WILL YOU NEED?

You will need two pieces of material, each the same size.
Length: Have someone measure you. Start at the shoulder and measure down to the point where you want the costume to end. This is the LENGTH OF YOUR COSTUME and the length each piece of fabric should be.
Width: Multiply the LENGTH by 2. This is the width each piece of fabric should be.

You will also need a tape measure, a pencil, scissors and needle and thread.

1. Lay out your two pieces of material.
2. Fold each piece of material in half from left to right.

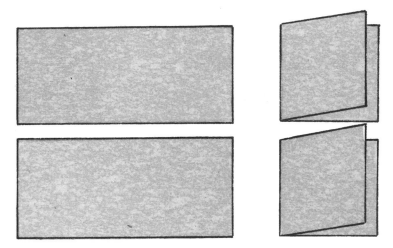

3. Measure and cut each folded piece of material separately. Place your tape measure with the zero at A. Measure and mark off the LENGTH OF YOUR COSTUME in several places.
4. Connect these points with a light, curved pencil line.
5. Cut through both layers of cloth along this line.

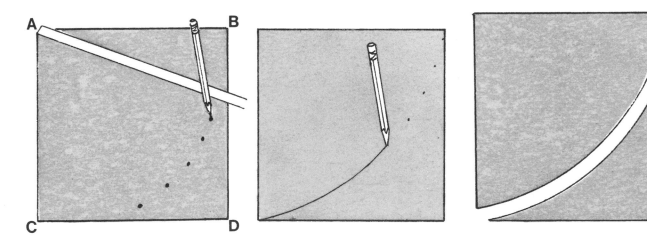

Before sewing the semicircles together, cut an opening for your head:

6. Leave your material folded and place the tape measure with the zero at A again. Measure and mark off a length of 3 inches in several places.

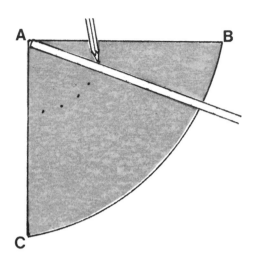

7. Connect these points with a light, curved pencil line.
8. Cut along this line. Unfold both pieces of material.

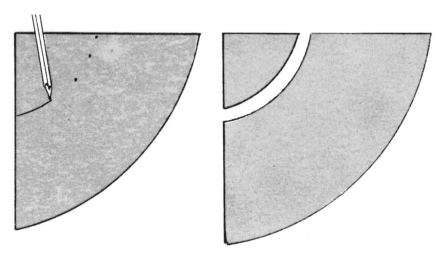

If your circle is going to be completely closed, then just sew the two semicircles together:

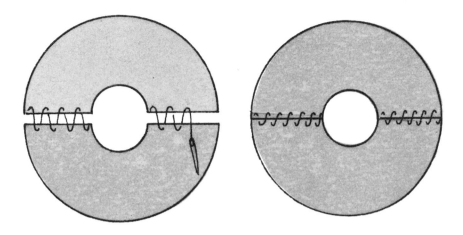

If you are making a circle to use as a cape, use the fact that you are working with two pieces of material to your advantage, and save yourself some sewing. Join the semicircles on one side of the neckline only. Leave the other side free. This free side will serve as the opening in the front of your cape. You may fasten this with a string or brooch (see page 81).

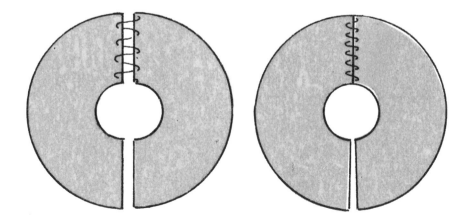

2 How to Make the T

Stand in front of a mirror with your knees pressed together and your arms stretched out straight from your shoulders. This is the T. The T-shaped gown was worn by kings, monks, peasant women, noblewomen, bishops, court jesters and many others. The T can be worn perfectly STRAIGHT, as in the drawing of the king's costume, or it can be ANGLED, as in the drawing of the sorcerer's costume, where the skirt of the dress flares out at the bottom. The T can be long, like the noblewoman's costume, or short, like Robin Hood's. And for additional variety the sleeves can be STRAIGHT, as they are on the knight's costume, or ANGLED, like the monk's. The T was practical, comfortable, and obviously versatile.

WHAT SIZE PIECE OF MATERIAL WILL YOU NEED?

You will be making the front, the back and the sleeves of your costume from one piece of material.

Length: Have someone measure you. Measure from your shoulder down to the point where you want your costume to end. Multiply this number by 2. This is the length your piece of material should be.

Width: For a costume with long sleeves, use a piece of material 54 inches wide. For a costume with elbow-length sleeves use a piece of material 36 inches wide.

Besides the material, you will need a tape measure, a pencil, scissors, straight pins and a needle and thread.

1. Lay out your piece of material.

2. Fold your material in half from top to bottom,
3. and in half again from left to right. The fold in the material should be on your left.

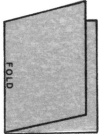

4. Have someone measure across your chest from under one arm to under the other. *Divide the total in half and add one.* This is the WIDTH.

5. Place your tape measure along the line we have called AB and measure and mark off the WIDTH.

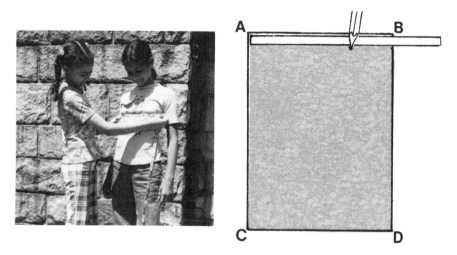

6. Place your tape measure along the line we have called CD. FOR A STRAIGHT T: Measure and mark off the WIDTH. FOR AN ANGLED T: Measure and mark off the WIDTH plus 9 inches.

7. Connect these points with a straight, light pencil line. We will call this line you have just drawn EF.

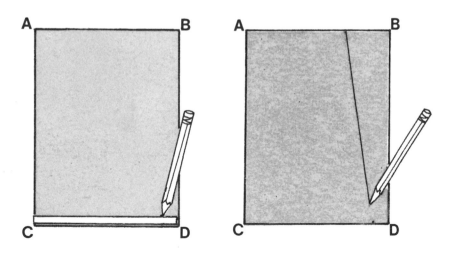

TO MEASURE FOR SLEEVES

8. Place your tape measure along line EF and measure 9 inches down from the top. Call this point G.

9. Place your tape measure along line BD. FOR STRAIGHT SLEEVES: Measure and mark off 9 inches down from the top. FOR ANGLED SLEEVES: Measure and mark off 13 inches down. This is point H.

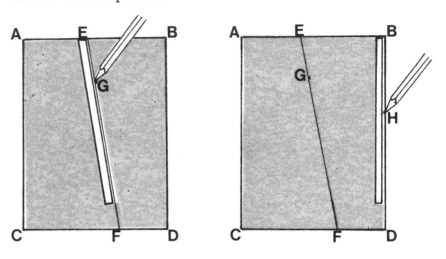

10. Connect points G and H with a straight, light pencil line.

11. Carefully cut out the T by cutting from H to G to F.

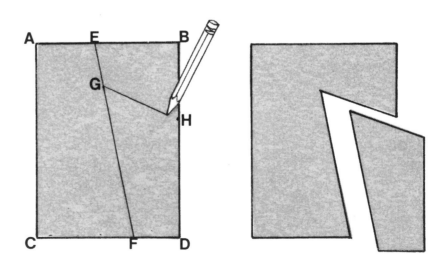

TO CUT AN OPENING FOR YOUR HEAD

12. Leave the material folded and place your tape measure at A. Measure and mark off a length of 3 inches in several places.

13. Connect these points with a curved, light pencil line. Cut along this line.

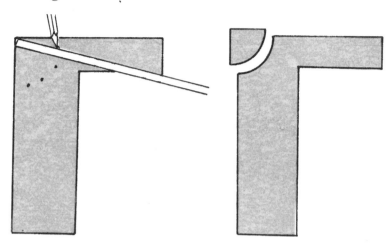

TO FINISH THE T

14. Unfold the T and try it on. Cut the ends of the sleeves if they are too long. Check the length of the costume.

15. Take off the T. Lay it out with the front neatly folded over the back and pin the front and the back together along the sleeves and down each side. Leave the openings for your hands, the bottom and the neckline free. Sew the T where you have pinned it.

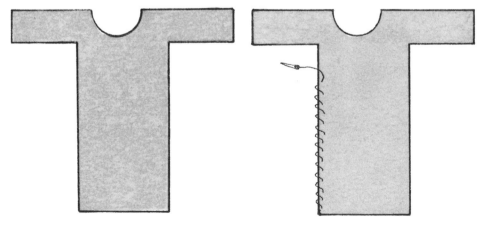

3   How to Make the Tunic

The knight wore a TUNIC made out of metal to protect him against an opponent, and the peasant wore a tunic made out of wool to protect him against the cold. The TUNIC has a lower neckline than the T and is sleeveless. Like the T, it can be worn either STRAIGHT or ANGLED. In the Middle Ages it was considered indecent to expose one's elbows in public, and the sleeveless TUNIC was sometimes worn under a cape and always worn over a T-shaped gown.

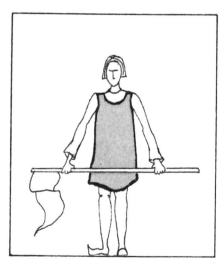 

WHAT SIZE PIECE OF MATERIAL WILL YOU NEED?

Length: Have someone measure you. Measure from your shoulder to the point where you want your costume to end. Multiply this number by 2. This is the length your piece of material should be.

Width: Use a piece of material 36 inches wide.

Besides the fabric you will need a tape measure, a pencil and scissors.

1. Lay out your piece of material.
2. Fold your material in half from top to bottom,
3. and in half again from left to right. The fold in your material should be on the left-hand side.

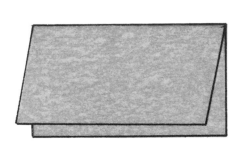

FOLD

4. Have someone measure across your chest from under one arm to under the other. Divide the total in half and add one. This is the WIDTH.
5. Place your tape measure along line AB and measure and mark off the WIDTH.

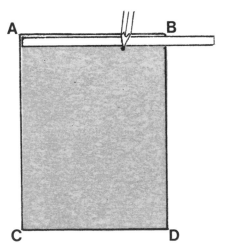

A   B

C   D

6. Place your tape measure along line CD. FOR A STRAIGHT TUNIC: Measure and mark off the WIDTH. FOR AN ANGLED TUNIC: Measure and mark off the WIDTH plus 5 inches.

7. Connect these two points with a straight, light pencil line. Carefully cut out the tunic along this line.

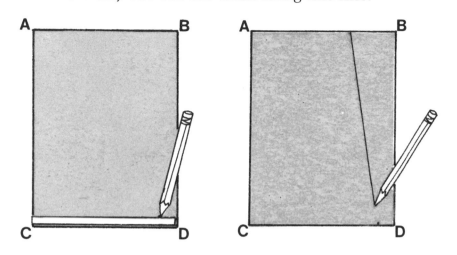

TO CUT AN OPENING FOR YOUR HEAD

8. Leave your material folded. Place your tape measure at A.

9. If the WIDTH is 8 inches or less: Measure and mark off a length of 3½ inches in several places. If the WIDTH is more than 8 inches: Measure and mark off a length of 4 inches in several places.

10. Connect these points with a light, curved pencil line.

11. Cut along this line. Unfold the material.

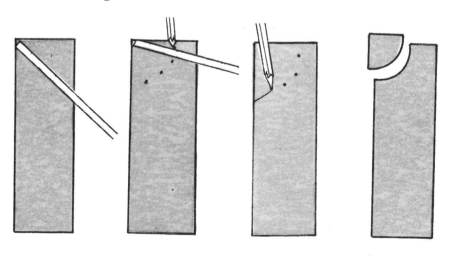

✤MEDIEVAL CHARACTERS

HOW TO CHOOSE A MEDIEVAL CHARACTER

If you are making a costume for a play then you have an assigned part and you know which medieval character you want to make a costume for. But if you are going to a costume party, or are going to be in a parade or a festival, then you can choose to be any character who lived in medieval times. Certain choices come to mind immediately—a queen, a noblewoman, a knight, a sorcerer. But there were heralds, minstrels, merchants and a whole group of other interesting medieval characters to choose from. Notice in the photographs that girls as well as boys choose to be sorcerers, minstrels and jesters. A woman had fewer choices for the Middle Ages, but you can choose to be any character you want to be. Read through the following section to find out about these chracters, what their jobs were and how they dressed.

If your whole class is making costumes, remember that more than one person can choose the same character. Two people can be craftsmen; one can be a baker, for instance, the other a blacksmith. If there's to be more than one minstrel you can form a band of minstrels, with one singer, one storyteller and one musician. You can even have more than one king and queen; just make one person the king of one country and the other the king of a different country.

KING

The king was the richest and most important person in the country. He could make laws, levy taxes and start wars. This was true while a man was king, but to remain king he had to have the help and loyalty of his nobles and his knights. The job of "king" was usually inherited, but without nobles to run the estates and knights to protect his property the king would have lost his kingdom.

How the king looked and dressed influenced all those at court. Long hair, once a source of pride and vanity, became unfashionable the day Henry I of England cut his. And although the greatest jewels and most opulent fabrics were available to him, the king did not always choose to dress lavishly. As an act of humility Louis IX of France refused to wear extravagant fashions. Richard the Lionhearted, who wore magnificent robes and gold sandals for his coronation, wisely chose protection over pomp in dressing to fight in the Crusades. And Henry II of England was just more interested in comfort than elegance. But a king was aware that his clothes reflected his importance, and for ceremonial occasions he usually wore the most elegant and costly clothes in his country.

King Arthur. Detail from one of
The Nine Heroes Tapestries,
probably by Nicholas Bataille
French, ca. 1385.

To make a costume for a king, imagine him on a ceremonial occasion and dress in full regalia, with a coronation robe.

TO MAKE THE GOWN

Make a long STRAIGHT T with STRAIGHT sleeves. You can decorate this gown with an overall pattern or a heraldic design on the front. A heraldic design is a picture or symbol which a medieval person adopted as his emblem. Each person chose a unique design and no one else, except members of his family, could use the exact same design. Knights used these designs on their shields and tunics, and kings, nobles and guildsmen used them to decorate their costumes. King Arthur, appropriately enough, chose a picture of a crown, to symbolize his royalty. For more information about heraldic designs see page 59.

For a belt, use a strip of leather or fabric and decorate it with jewels and a fancy belt buckle (see page 81).

TO MAKE THE ROBE

To make a regal robe, make a CIRCLE which is the same length as your gown. Cut an opening for your head. Cut the front of the circle open (or if you made semicircles sew only one seam) and plan to fasten it at the neckline with a jeweled brooch or pin (page 81). This cape can be worn open straight down the middle of your body, or you can fasten the cape over your right shoulder and show off a colorful lining.

TO MAKE A LINING

Use a lighter-weight fabric than you used for the robe. Fabric stores sell inexpensive, shiny material that looks like satin for lining coats and dresses, which is perfect for lining a royal robe. Your lining material must be the exact same size as the piece of material you used for the robe. Make a CIRCLE and cut an opening for your head. Cut the circle open down the front. Lay out the robe and place the lining exactly on top of it. Pin the lining in place and then sew it to the robe.

To make the robe especially opulent you can trim it with fake fur. Use a furlike material to trim the edges of the robe and make a wide fur collar.

TO MAKE A FUR COLLAR

You will need an 18-inch-square piece of material. Make a CIRCLE, using 9 inches as the length. Cut an opening for your head and slit the circle open down the front. Stitch the fur collar around the neckline of the robe.

You can make a king's scepter (see page 108), and naturally your costume must be topped off with an elaborate gold crown (page 83).

QUEEN

To form a friendship between their two countries, the king of one country sometimes offered his daughter's hand in marriage to the king of another country. Such a marriage created a peaceful bond between the two nations; the father felt secure that his daughter's husband would not declare war on her old homeland, and likewise, the husband felt secure that his wife's father would not attack her new homeland. The queen was just a token exchange between the two nations, and it didn't matter whether she liked her new husband or he liked her. This new queen introduced the customs and clothing of her homeland to her new court. For instance, Isabella of Bavaria not only brought herself and the goodwill of her people to France when she married Charles VI in 1385, she also brought along a new hat, called the hennin.

Traveling was difficult in the Middle Ages, and the queen rarely left the confines of her castle and court, and of course, there were no newspapers or magazines in the Middle Ages. But even though most people never saw the queen, she was a fashion trend setter. Noblewomen imitated the queen, and when merchants' wives saw what the noblewomen were wearing they imitated them, and so on, down the ranks of medieval society. But although they fancied a new gown or cape, medieval people valued the beauty and quality of their old clothing, and queens and noblewomen often bequeathed their favorite dresses to their daughters.

TO MAKE A GOWN

Make a long ANGLED T gown. The gown can have STRAIGHT, ANGLED or any of the sleeves suggested in the description of the noblewoman's costume (page 28). Your costume must be very rich-looking, and if it is to be worn

The tapestry King Solomon and the Queen of Sheba *German, 15th century.*

in a play where someone else will be cast as a noble-woman, you must make sure that the queen's dress is more luxurious. One way to do this is to decorate the bottom of each noblewoman's dress with a band of fur and use a wider band on the queen's dress. Or attach trains of fabric at the shoulder of each gown and make the queen's train longer. Decorate the dress with an overall pattern or a heraldic emblem (page 59) on the front of the gown. If you will be wearing your costume in a pageant or play where someone will portray the king, you should both use the same emblem on your gowns.

TO MAKE A CAPE

Make a cape from a long CIRCLE. The cape should be open down the front and fastened with a brooch (page 81).

TO MAKE A FUR OR VELVET COLLAR
FOR THE QUEEN'S CAPE

Use a 12-inch-square piece of material to make a CIRCLE. (The length of the circle is 6 inches.) Cut an opening for your head and cut the circle open down the front. Stitch the collar to the neckline of the cape.

Make a crown to wear with your costume (page 83).

NOBLEWOMAN

The noblewoman lived in a castle or a manor. She supervised the many servants, and made sure that everything ran smoothly in the castle. When her husband was traveling on business, fighting in the Crusades, or away from home for any long period of time, the noblewoman took over his duties and ran the entire estate.

She studied embroidery, weaving and sewing, and was taught to compose poetry and sing songs. The noblewoman was married by the time she was fourteen to a man chosen by her father. She had few legal rights; until she was married she "belonged" to her father and after her marriage she "belonged" to her husband. As a symbol of this ownership she wore her husband's coat of arms (heraldic design) on her dress.

She wore beautiful clothes and costly jewels to show off her wealth. To outshine rival noblewomen, she would try to wear higher hats and longer trains than they did. Sometimes this resulted in hats which were so high and so large that the noblewoman couldn't walk through her castle doorway! Agnes Sorel, a girl friend of Charles VII of France, thought up a clever trick for the noblewoman to differentiate her rank from all others. Noblewomen began trimming the bottoms of their dresses with bands of fur, and the noblewoman with the highest rank wore the widest band.

TO MAKE A GOWN

A noblewoman must wear a luxurious costume. Make a long ANGLED T gown decorated with an overall pattern, or a coat of arms (page 59). If you are making a costume for a play or pageant where someone else will portray your husband, you should each decorate your costumes with the same coat of arms. Your gown can have STRAIGHT or ANGLED sleeves. A variety of sleeves was popular in the Middle Ages, some of them lined with fabric of another color, and you can choose any one of the following styles for your costume:

Notice the noblewoman's winged headdress. Detail from a tapestry, Lady with a Falcon Sitting in a Flowery Grove
Franco-Flemish, 1420-1435.

1. pictures the noblewoman's gown with ANGLED sleeves (see page 14).

2. The back of this sleeve is longer than the front. Measure for ANGLED sleeves and cut out the T. Place your tape measure along line AB and measure 6 inches in from B toward A. We will call this point I.

Connect point I to point H, the lower right-hand corner of the sleeve, with a curved line, as show in the illustration. Cut along this curved line.

3. This is a scalloped sleeve. Follow the instructions for sleeve 2, but connect points I and H with a *wavy, scalloped* line. Cut along the scalloped line.

The inside of the sleeve shows in both of these styles, and for extra effect you can line the insides of the sleeves with a different-colored fabric.

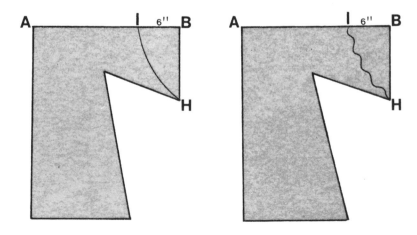

4. The streamer at the end of this sleeve is called a *tippet*. Measure for STRAIGHT sleeves and cut out the T. Sew a streamer of long material, 3 to 6 inches wide, to the cuff of each sleeve.

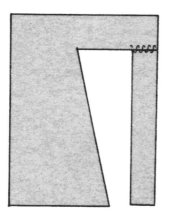

TO LINE THE SLEEVES OF YOUR GOWN

Before you sew the T together, open the T and place a sleeve on the fabric you have chosen for the lining.
Trace the shape of the sleeve onto the fabric and cut it out.
Do the same for the second sleeve.
Sew the lining onto the insides of the sleeves.

TO MAKE A CAPE

To make a cape to wear with your costume, make a CIRCLE the same length as the gown. Cut the circle open down the front and fasten the cape with a brooch (page 81), or cut two 12-inch pieces of ribbon and sew one to each side of the neckline to be used as ties to close the cape.

You can make a medallion (page 82) or a pouch (page 106), and be sure to make a winged headdress (page 93), hennin (page 98) or circlet (page 101) to complete the noblewoman's costume.

NOBLEMAN

The nobleman governed an estate which was sometimes as large as a whole kingdom. The more land the nobleman acquired, the more powerful he was; but as he acquired more land the nobleman also acquired more responsibilities. He had to feed, clothe and house the serfs who worked his land, as well as the cooks, maids and many servants it took to run his manor. He also had to provide food, lodging and a change of clothing for the frequent overnight guests who visited his estate, and of course there were his wife and children who had to be well provided for. One sign of the nobleman's wealth was the quality of the clothing he provided for his servants.

The greatest sign of the nobleman's wealth, however, was the clothing he wore himself. His clothes were made

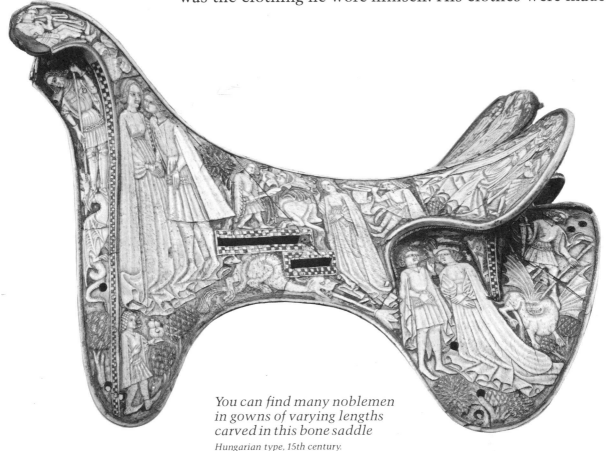

You can find many noblemen in gowns of varying lengths carved in this bone saddle
Hungarian type, 15th century.

from the finest fabrics, and he <u>wore</u> jeweled brooches, belt buckles, medallions and rings. The nobleman believed that it was his birthright to wear extravagant fashions, and when merchants and guildsmen were earning enough money to be able to purchase luxurious fashions for themselves, the noblemen passed laws forbidding them to do so. These "sumptuary laws" decreed that no matter what you could afford, certain clothes were proper only for certain classes. English sumptuary laws forbade tradesmen and merchants from buying silk and wearing gold jewelry. Craftsmen were permitted to wear lamb, rabbit or fox fur, but could not buy sable or ermine. But sumptuary laws were impossible to enforce because merchants, eager to sell goods, didn't care who bought them, and jewels, furs and fine fabrics became available to anyone who could afford them.

Women's dresses remained long throughout the period, but toward the end of the Middle Ages short gowns for men became fashionable. This gives you a choice in making the nobleman's costume.

TO MAKE A GOWN

You can make either a long STRAIGHT T gown with STRAIGHT or ANGLED sleeves, or a short ANGLED T with ANGLED sleeves which ends about six inches above your knees. The short T is especially appropriate if you are making a costume for a young nobleman, and if you choose the short T plan to wear it over a pair of colored tights and make a pair of medieval shoes (see page 104). Whichever gown you make should be richly decorated with an overall pattern or a coat of arms (page 59).

You can make a CIRCLE the same length as your gown to wear as a cape. Cut the circle open down the front and fasten the cape with a jeweled brooch (page 81). Add jewelry to your costume, and perhaps a pouch (page 106) tied around your waist; and be sure to make the floppy man's hat (page 86).

BISHOP

Nobles were powerful because they owned land. When a nobleman died his land was inherited by his eldest son, leaving his younger sons without any property of their own. Some of these younger sons became knights, and others joined the church and became bishops so they would regain power by ruling over the serfs and land owned by the church.

The basic costume of the clergy was the long, T-shaped gown, and as the noble's contrasted with the peasant's, the bishop's costume was more elegant than the priest's because it was made out of more luxurious materials. Look at this fifteenth-century painting (from left to right the clergy pictured are Benedict, Francis, Sylvester and Anthony Abbot) and you can immediately tell who the most important churchman is. They all wear the T, but Benedict's is made from a coarse piece of burlap material while Sylvester's T is shiny velvet. The least important of the four, Benedict and Francis, do not have cloaks to wear, and to make sure that Sylvester looks more impressive than Anthony, his cloak is decorated with jewels and fastened with an elaborate clasp. Sylvester is the only one who wears any jewelry. And while the others go bareheaded, Sylvester wears a tall, impressive hat which points toward heaven.

The clothes worn by the clergy were called vestments. The bishop wore three pieces of clothing: an alb, a chasuble and a cope, or, to us, a T, a TUNIC and a CIRCLE.

Madonna and Child Enthroned with Saints and Angels. *Tempera on wood by Francesco Botticini* Italian, ca. 1446-1497.

TO MAKE AN ALB

Use white material to make a long STRAIGHT T with STRAIGHT sleeves for the alb. The alb will be worn under the chasuble and the cope and should be made of a lightweight fabric (a cotton sheet is good) so your costume doesn't look or feel too bulky.

TO MAKE A CHASUBLE

Make a STRAIGHT TUNIC which ends at your thigh for the chasuble. Decorate the chasuble with a tablon (see page 58). Cut the square edges off the bottom of the tunic to make a round bottom.

TO MAKE A COPE

Make an ankle-length CIRCLE for the cope. The cope has a wide opening down the front so you can see the chasuble under it. Measure and cut out the circle and an opening for your head.

TO CUT A WIDE OPENING DOWN THE FRONT OF THE CIRCLE

1. Leave the circle folded in half. Draw a line down the middle of this semicircle, where the second fold was.
2. Measure 1 inch from this line on both sides of the neckline. Measure 3 inches from this line on both sides of the bottom.

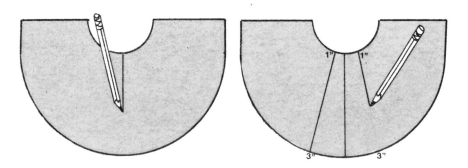

3. Connect each of the two points at the neckline with the point below it on the hem. Cutting only the top layer of material, cut along these two lines you have just drawn.

4. Cut a strip of material 4 inches wide and 2 inches long. Measure 8 inches down from the neckline of the cope toward the bottom. Sew the strip of material to the inside of the cope at the point you have just measured, attaching it on both sides of the open front. This strip of material across your chest will hold the cope in place when you wear it.

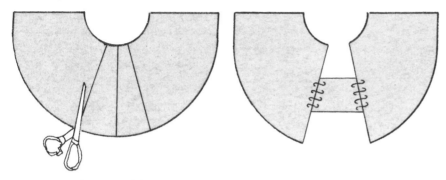

Trim the neckline, edges and bottom of the cope with embroidered ribbon.

The bishop carries a crosier (see page 110) and wears a hat called a miter (page 96).

Saint Gaul with a Bear. *Stained glass German, 16th century.*

MONK

Monk. Detail from a stone tomb slab French, 14th century.

While the bishop led the rich life of a noble, most monks took a vow of poverty and led a strict and simple life at a monastery. The monastery was secluded from the outside world. Here the monk followed an unchanging daily routine of prayer, study and work within the walls of the monastery. Boys from noble families rarely chose this way of life, but to boys from poor families life at the monastery had advantages. Monks were clothed, housed and fed, and they lived peaceful lives. Often boys who became monks had attended schools run by the monastery. Sometimes parents would give a newborn baby to the monastery because they could not afford to feed him. They knew that at the monastery the child would be well cared for and have the opportunity to receive an education, which they could never give him.

Monks were among the few people in the Middle Ages who could read and write. There were no printing presses until the fifteenth century, and books had to be handwritten. It was a laborious chore, but medieval monks copied texts from the Bible and from literature and history books. It was such a time-consuming task that it could take a monk's whole lifetime just to recopy one book. If the monks had not transcribed these books, we probably would not have copies of anything written before the fifteenth century.

The monk wore simple clothes. He wore a coarse wool gown with a cowl collar. This was called a "habit." Monks at the same monastery all wore the same color habit. There was an order of monks in the Middle Ages who wore white habits, but more typically the monks dressed in either black or brown.

TO MAKE A HABIT

Use wool, burlap or felt to make a long ANGLED T with ANGLED sleeves. The monk's habit was roomy, so make the T wider than the instructions call for.

To make a wider T, follow the instructions for making the T up to step 5, when you measure the width. Divide that total in half and add two. Use this number as the WIDTH and follow the rest of the instructions as written.

The wide collar on the monk's gown was called a cowl. Use the same fabric you did for the T, and:

TO MAKE A COWL COLLAR

Use an 18-inch-square piece of fabric to make a CIRCLE. The length of the circle is 9 inches. Leave the circle folded.

1. To cut an opening for your head, measure and mark two arcs: one using a 2-inch length and the other using a 3-inch length.

2. Cut along the 2-inch arc.

3. Measure and mark straight lines connecting the neckline and the arc drawn below it. Make the lines approximately 2 inches apart. Cut along these lines. You now have 2-inch-wide strips, or tabs.

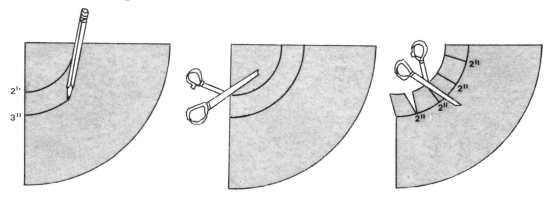

4. Place the collar over the T and line up the necklines.

5. Fold the tabs and pin them around the neckline on the inside of the gown. After you have pinned the tabs, use a needle and thread to sew them to the gown. The tabs give a little more weight to the neckline and help make the collar stand away from the gown.

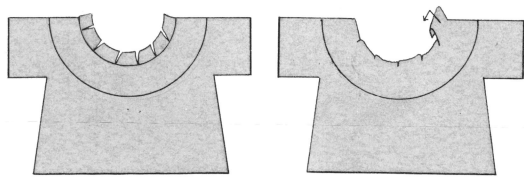

Use a thick piece of twine or rope tied around the waist of the gown for a belt.

KNIGHT

Shirt of mail German. 15th century.

The most romantic figure of the Middle Ages is the knight. We picture him fighting a great battle or rescuing a damsel in distress. The knight lived by a code of chivalry, and he pledged to be gallant and courteous, and to abide by the rules of fair play. The knight captured the fancy of many medieval ladies, and he was the object of poems and love stories. The knight is the medieval character most people would like to be.

Most knights came from noble families. If a boy wanted to become a knight he entered the household of a feudal lord when he was ten or eleven years old. He served as a page in the household and studied archery, fencing, hunting and sports, and read literature and poetry. After four years he was promoted to the rank of squire, and he could accompany the lord into battle. Knights fought on horseback and the squire had to learn to ride and handle his horse expertly. If after ten years of training, at the age of twenty-one, he met all of the requirements, he became a knight.

The knight needed clothes that would protect him in battle. He wore a shirt of mail. Mail was made of small interlocking circles of steel, and the shirt that the knight wore weighed about twenty-five pounds. He wore a shirt underneath the mail so the cold steel would not be up against his skin. Over the mail the knight wore a metal breastplate and backplate, and toward the end of the Middle Ages his whole body was encased in armor.

To protect his head the knight wore a helmet which covered his whole face. Because his face was covered it was impossible to identify individual knights; after all, one man wearing armor looks pretty much like another. So the knight painted a symbol on his shield. Each knight used different colors and different designs and could be recognized by his shield. The idea of having a symbol or emblem gained popularity, and soon nobles, and even merchants, were creating their own designs. These designs were called heraldry.

TO MAKE A SHIRT

Use a pattern for the STRAIGHT T with STRAIGHT sleeves to make a waist-length mail shirt. Try to find a material which is silver mesh or looks like metal. If you can't, choose a nubby-textured knit fabric, make the T, and then spray paint the shirt silver.

TO MAKE A TUNIC

You can make a metal breastplate and backplate (see page 74) to wear over the mail shirt or a TUNIC. If you make a TUNIC, it can be six inches above your knees or knee length. Decorate the front of the tunic with a coat of arms (a form of a heraldic design) (page 59) and belt the tunic with a 3-inch-wide strip of leather or fabric, knotted in the front.

The knight's helmet is described on page 89.

You should make a shield (see page 79) and decorate it with the same coat of arms you used on your tunic or breastplate. You can also make a sword (page 78) to be tucked into your belt.

Tomb effigy of Jean D'Alluye, a knight. Carved stone French, 13th century.

HERALD

With so many people adopting heraldic symbols and emblems, someone had to remember what all the different symbols stood for and whom they identified. This was the job of the herald.

The herald accompanied armies of knights into battle. He identified dead knights by the symbols on their shields, and acted as a courier when the knights wanted to send messages to the enemy. The herald wore a colorful costume called a tabard so that he would not be mistaken for a soldier when he approached the enemy's camp. There was no mail service in the Middle Ages, and the herald served as a messenger in peacetime as well. When he delivered a letter he carried a small badge bearing his employer's coat of arms to prove who had sent him.

TO MAKE A TABARD

Make a knee-length ANGLED T with ANGLED sleeves. The herald's tabard was divided, checkerboard fashion, into four sections on the front and four sections on the back, and a heraldic symbol was used to decorate each section. Make one heraldic design and repeat it in each of the sections, or choose several different designs to decorate your tabard.

Wear a pair of colored tights and medieval shoes (page 104) with your costume.

MERCHANT

The least prestigious merchant was the peddler who took his wares from town to town, but the true medieval "merchant" was a wealthy businessman who imported and exported exotic goods. The merchant imported the silk fabric from Florence, the wool from Flanders and the fine linen from Reims that the nobleman wanted for his clothing. He arranged for exotic spices and foods the noble could not get at home to be brought to him. The merchant had to find a source for these products, bargain for their purchase and see that they were safely delivered to his buyer. He demanded high fees for his service, and soon the merchant became wealthy enough to buy these luxuries for himself.

TO MAKE A GOWN

For a merchant make a long STRAIGHT T with STRAIGHT sleeves. Use rich-looking fabric, and decorate it with an overall pattern (page 53).

Over this gown the merchant wore a TUNIC.

TO MAKE THE MERCHANT'S TUNIC

Make a long STRAIGHT TUNIC. Sew up the sides of the tunic, leaving 11 inches from the shoulder down free on each side to slip your arms through. Cut the tunic open down the front. If you can find an imitation fur, use it to trim the neckline, bottom edge and armholes of the tunic.

Make a hat (page 86) and be sure to make a pouch (page 106), to hold all the merchant's money, to wear with your costume.

Merchant with a pouch. Detail from a tapestry, The Triumph of Time *Franco-Flemish, early 16th century.*

CRAFTSMEN

By the end of the Middle Ages many people had moved from farms and nobles' estates into towns. Travels in the Crusades introduced people to Oriental spices and fabrics, and trade routes were established with the East to import these exotic items. Great European fairs were held, at which goods from all over Europe and the East were bought and sold. More goods were available, and the demand for them also increased. The peasant who wove his own fabric, grew his own vegetables and shod his own horses barely had enough time to do all of those jobs for himself; he certainly couldn't grow enough extra vegetables or weave enough extra fabric to sell to others. But a man who did only one job could do that job more quickly than the peasant who divided his time among many different chores, and would be an expert at his trade. To meet the growing demand for products, workers began specializing in one trade; and to insure that they were well paid for their work they formed guilds.

Tanners, bakers, blacksmiths, goldsmiths, weavers and furriers; there was a guild for every craft and trade. The guild was a kind of union. It regulated the amount of money workers were paid and limited the number of people in a profession. Often you could join only if your father was a member. Daughters were sometimes admitted to sewing and weaving guilds, but most memberships were reserved for boys. Guild members trained their wives to help them with their work, and if a member died his wife was allowed to take over his membership in the guild. The guild set high standards for the work done by its members and created a rigid training system through which all of its members had to pass. An expert in a trade was a mastercraftsman. Youngsters accepted into the guild became apprentices and were assigned to the workshop of a mastercraftsman. An apprentice studied with this master for five or six years, after which time he took a test to become a journeyman. If he passed, the journeyman was allowed to travel around and work for other mastercraftsmen as an assistant. Before the journeyman could qualify as a mastercraftsman himself he had to pass still another test, and a finished piece of his work was judged by a committee of the guild.

Although the craftsman had more money than the peasant and he lived in a more comfortable house, the craftsman's clothing was the same as any workingman's: simple, warm, protective and suited to his job.

TO MAKE A GOWN

Choose a dark-colored fabric and make an ANGLED T with STRAIGHT sleeves. Angled sleeves interfered with work and were not worn on the job by any workers. For this same reason the craftsman's T is ankle length, not floor length. The T should end a few inches below your knees or at your ankle, and be tied at the waist with a belt. A mastercraftsman should have a coat of arms (page 59) which represents his guild on the front of his T. Journeymen and apprentices wear unadorned costumes.

Blacksmiths or bakers can wear a large rectangular apron tied around their waists. To show what kind of work the craftsman does, carry a prop as part of your costume. The mason could carry a trowel, the tailor a needle and thread, the blacksmith a horseshoe.

PEASANT

During any period in history, peasant costume had little to do with current fashions. In the Middle Ages the peasant wore whatever clothes he could get, and if he was lucky they were warm and lasted until he was able to get something else to wear. The peasant lived in the countryside, far away from the king's court, and if he was at all curious about what the nobility was wearing, his isolated life gave him no clue. Although peasants worked for the nobility, they actually saw little of them. The peasant spent most of his life working, and when he wasn't working he spent a lot of time in church, praying, trying to make sure that his afterlife would be better. Unlike her noble counterpart, the peasant woman was not a "valuable possession" to be traded by her father, and the peasant was usually free to marry for love.

The peasant did not wear a long T gown because it is not practical to work in floor-length clothes. The noble wore bright, gaudy colors; the peasant wore dark, somber ones. When the noble's clothes got dirty he changed into another outfit and let the dirty ones soak for several days in a bath of diluted warm wine. The peasant did not have other clothes to change into, and he washed what he wore with plain soap and water.

Peasant woman using mortar and pestle, peasant man sowing seeds. Woodcuts from Das Buch von Pflanzung der Aecker, Bäume und aller Kräuter *by Petrus de Crescentiis* German, 1512.

TO MAKE A GOWN

For the man's costume make an ANGLED T which ends a few inches below your knees, with STRAIGHT sleeves. Use a dark-colored felt or coarse material.

Much of the peasant's work was done outdoors, and it was important that his head be covered. Find a straw hat with a wide brim or make a hood (see page 88) to wear with your costume.

For the peasant woman make an ankle-length ANGLED T gown with STRAIGHT sleeves. If she was lucky, the peasant had a tunic to wear over this gown.

TO MAKE THE PEASANT'S TUNIC

Use burlap or any coarse material to make an ANGLED
TUNIC a few inches shorter than the peasant's gown. Sew
up the sides of the tunic, leaving 11 inches from the
shoulder down free on each side to slip your arms through.

The peasant woman might wear an apron improvised
from a large rectangle of material tied around her waist.
On her head she wore a straw hat, a hood (page 88) or a
piece of fabric tied over her hair.

Use props with your costume to show the work the
peasant did. Carry a staff for a shepherd, a scythe for a
farmer or an everyday household item, like a broom, a jug
or a basket.

SORCERER

The word "sorcerer" is magical itself and conjures up images as different as Merlin the Magician, the Sorcerer's Apprentice and Dr. Faust. Was the sorcerer a helpful magician who could get rid of sickness and change a person's luck, or was he an agent of the devil? The church preached against the use of magic and the clergy conducted witchhunts and trials. But people continued to seek the help of the sorcerer. In church you prayed for results you might or might not get later, but the sorcerer's help was immediate.

The sorcerer used amulets, charms, chants, herbs and magic spells to deal with problems of life, poverty, health and, of course, love. Some supposed sorcerers were scholars, and the magical works of Roger Bacon were actually discoveries in the science of chemistry. Perhaps the sorcerer couldn't make you rich or beautiful, but some of his "herb magic" was actually good medicine. Today we use a few of the salves and ointments made from plants which were used by witches and healers in the Middle Ages, and a competent witch might be just the person to see if you had a bad cut or bruise.

TO MAKE A GOWN

Make a long ANGLED T gown with extra-wide sleeves.

To make extra-wide sleeves follow the instructions for making the T through step 8, when you measure for the sleeves. After you measure and mark off 9 inches along line EF, measure and mark off 16 inches along line BD. Connect these two points with a light pencil line and cut out your gown.

Decorate your gown with bold designs, using the sun, the stars, the moon or other symbols of the universe the sorcerer might have used to invoke his powers.

Carry a magic wand (page 109), and wear an amulet or a lucky charm on a necklace. For extra drama, wear a long, flowing cape, made from a floor-length CIRCLE. Cut the circle open down the front and sew a 12-inch-long piece of ribbon to each side of the neckline to fasten the cape.

COURT JESTER

A knave, a fool, a joker; it's easy to imagine the court jester in his cap and bells pantomiming, juggling or just acting silly to make the king and his court laugh. But his nicknames are misleading, for the court jester was not a "fool" who did "silly" things—he was an entertainer and held an official post at court. It was not uncommon for wealthy people other than the king to employ jesters— nobles, and sometimes bishops, had jesters on their household staffs.

The court jester was on constant call to provide entertainment at the castle. He danced, sang, mimed, did acrobatics and often made outrageous, and sometimes rude, jokes. His humor was a useful tool to the king, and the court jester's jokes often masked serious comments on the life and politics of the court. His colorful dagged-edged costume was an exaggeration of the clothes worn by everyday people. His costume was parti-colored (the right side one color and the left side another) and decorated with bells.

Brass candleholder in the shape of a jester, attributed to Aert van Tricht German, ca. 1500.

TO MAKE THE JESTER'S SUIT

For a court jester make an ANGLED T with ANGLED sleeves which ends about 6 inches above your knees. Cut dagged (pointed) edges around the bottom of the T and around the cuffs of the sleeves, and attach small metal bells to these points.

MAKING A PARTI-COLORED COSTUME requires some extra sewing. Instead of making the costume from one piece of material you will make the front and the back of the T separately. Choose two different and bright solid-color pieces of material. The jester costume has long sleeves, so the width of each piece should be 54 inches. Measure from your shoulder down to a point 6 inches above your knees to find the length.

Each piece of material should be this length, not doubled as in the usual T. Fold each piece *left to right only*, not top to bottom. Measure, mark and cut each piece separately,

following the instructions for making the ANGLED T with ANGLED sleeves, and remember to cut an opening for your head.

Keep each of these two pieces folded in half from left to right and cut along the fold.

From the four pieces of material you will now have, sew together two different-colored pieces for the front of the costume and two different-colored pieces for the back.

Cut dagged edges at the bottom of each piece and around the sleeves. Sew the front and the back of your costume together at the sides and along the sleeves.

Attach bells to the dagged points around the sleeves and the borders.

Wear a pair of colored tights with your costume, and make a pair of elongated, floppy shoes (page 104). Also make a jester's cap (see page 101) and "fool's head" (page 111)—these are trademarks of the court jester's costume and "musts" to complete your outfit.

MINSTREL

The minstrel went from town to town singing ballads and folk tunes. Few minstrels could read or write music, but they repeated songs taught to them by their fathers and invented tunes of their own. The minstrels recorded history in their songs about love, legends and battles, and many of the stories we now have written down about medieval times are known to us through the texts of their songs. The minstrel was welcomed wherever he went because he brought news of other towns and entertainment to the places at which he stopped.

The minstrel was "on the road" and his clothes were not always clean or in good condition, but he was an entertainer, and they were colorful.

Minstrel. Detail from a bone saddle Hungarian type, 15th century.

TO MAKE A MINSTREL'S SUIT

Make a knee-length ANGLED T with ANGLED sleeves. Add a few colorful patches to show that the minstrel's costume was well worn. You can attach bells or colorful streamers of material to your costume and make a scalloped collar.

TO MAKE A SCALLOPED COLLAR

Use the same material as the T or choose a contrasting color. Use a 24-inch square of material to make a CIRCLE. (The length of the circle is 12 inches.) Cut an opening for your head. Cut a wavy, scalloped line around the edge of the collar. Slip the collar on top of the T.

Wear a pair of colored tights and medieval shoes (page 104) with your costume. You can also make a hood (page 88) and carry a prop, such as a flute.

ROBIN HOOD

Robin Hood was a popular character in medieval ballads and stories. Minstrels traveled from town to town reciting the adventures of this legendary figure who "robbed from the rich to give to the poor," and even today, Robin remains a favorite folk hero. Robin Hood lived in Sherwood Forest with Maid Marian and his band of men, robbing rich nobles who traveled through the forest and outwitting the Sheriff of Nottingham.

TO MAKE ROBIN HOOD'S COSTUME

A woodsman, Robin Hood is always pictured wearing a green outfit, which provides him with good camouflage in the forest. Use green felt and make a STRAIGHT T with STRAIGHT elbow-length sleeves. The T should end about 6 inches above your knees. Cut uneven, dagged edges around the sleeves and bottom of the T. Use a 3-inch-wide strip of leather or felt and tie it around the front of the costume as a belt. The T should be worn over a pair of green or brown tights and with a pair of medieval shoes (page 104). Robin Hood was a noted archer, and you can carry a bow and arrow with your costume. Make the triangular cap (see page 103) which is traditionally associated with Robin Hood's costume.

To costume the other characters in this legend:

MAID MARIAN

Make a simple, long ANGLED T with STRAIGHT sleeves.

FRIAR TUCK

See the directions for the MONK's costume (page 36).

THE SHERIFF OF NOTTINGHAM

The Sheriff was a noble and should wear a long STRAIGHT T with STRAIGHT sleeves and a cape.

LITTLE JOHN AND THE REST OF ROBIN HOOD'S BAND OF MEN

Make STRAIGHT T gowns with STRAIGHT sleeves for these characters. The T's should be mid-thigh length and belted with pieces of felt, strips of leather or pieces of rope. Their clothing was tattered from the life they led in the forest, and you can put patches on your costume or "dirty it up." Wear a pair of tights and make a pair of medieval shoes (page 104) from felt or burlap.

✤DECORATING YOUR COSTUME

PLANNING YOUR DESIGN

When you add decorations and accessories to your costume it is important for them to look authentically medieval and be "in character" with the costume you are making. It would be just as out of place to dress a court jester in a drab, lifeless costume as it would be to dress a peasant in a colorful, bejeweled gown. Some characters wear costumes that have traditional designs associated with them, like the knight whose tunic bears a heraldic emblem. Others, like the noblewoman, wear richly decorated costumes, and it is up to you to provide appropriate fabric designs. Typical medieval designs are described on the following pages.

In thinking about decorating your costume, consider where to add the decoration. On the front, on the back, at the collar, cuffs and bottom or over all—any of these, singly or in combination, are good places to use patterns. The nobleman might wear a coat of arms on his T, and the bottom and cuffs of his costume might be decorated with a geometric border. The merchant could wear a tunic and a gown, each decorated with a different overall pattern.

If you are going to use more than one design, or decorate more than one piece of your costume, think about the total effect. Do the colors and designs look well together? Will all of your efforts be seen? It is silly to make an elaborate, time-consuming design on your gown if it is going to be completely covered by your cape.

Before you choose the type of medieval design you would like to make, read about stenciling, appliqué and hand painting and choose the most appropriate method for applying the design to your costume. Also read about the medieval adornments which can be added to your costume.

TYPES OF DESIGN

Geometric Designs

The simplest patterns used on medieval clothes were geometric. Throughout history people have used geometric designs to decorate fabrics. In the Middle Ages geometric shapes were often used in a checkerboard pattern: Rows and rows of the same geometric shape were drawn, and filled in with two alternating colors:

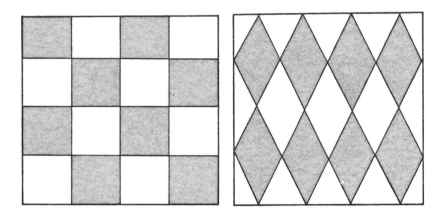

Another common geometric shape was the "stepped form" which looked like the parapets around the top of the castle:

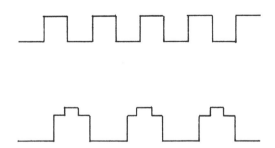

Geometric shapes are also very effective as backgrounds for other designs:

They also make good border designs for collars, cuffs and bottoms of costumes.

TO MAKE A BORDER DESIGN

Draw a geometric design around the edges of your costume, or apply the geometric design to a separate strip of fabric and sew the decorated strip to the collar, cuff or bottom of a gown, or down both sides of the front opening of a cape.

Animal and Flower Designs

The things people see around them are always good sources for designs. Medieval people loved bright, beautiful colors, and they copied the flowers that grew in their gardens and the birds and animals they saw in their woods. They attached symbolic meanings to some of the flowers and animals they chose. For instance, a picture of a fox represented cunning, an eagle stood for power and the camel, which was known as the "ship of the desert," represented endurance.

Animals, birds and flowers are good shapes to use in "repeat patterns." A repeat or "overall" pattern is one that is used to cover a whole piece of material.

TO MAKE A REPEAT PATTERN

Select the shape or shapes you want to use and make drawings of them.

Think about how you want to position these shapes on your costume. Where you place the shape on your costume can add variety to your design.

You can repeat the pattern very close together on the fabric: Or far apart:

You can arrange the pattern in neat rows:

Or scatter it randomly on the fabric:

You can also position the pattern in different directions to make a more intricate design:

Not all the animals that appear in medieval designs were copied from nature. Many were mythological or imaginary creatures. A favorite was the unicorn, which had the body of a horse, a horn on its head and a lion's tail, and was recognized as a symbol of purity. Another popular creature was Pegasus, the "flying horse" from Greek mythology. And of course the most terrifying monster of all imaginary animals was the fire-breathing dragon.

These beasts and creatures can be used in repeat patterns, and are especially good designs for large emblems or coats of arms. Look for pictures of birds and animals in books and magazines, and use flowers and animals in your neighborhood as models for your drawings. Or create an imaginary plant or animal which uses parts of real flowers and animals or is totally made up.

Tablons

Gardens, feasts and scenes of the hunt were popular medieval designs. People hand painted or embroidered these pictures of everyday scenes on pieces of material and sewed the material to the fronts of their costumes. These round or square designs were called tablons. Bishops wore designs which depicted religious stories.

TO MAKE A TABLON

Design a scene and paint or appliqué it onto a large piece of either square or round material. Sew the finished tablon onto the front of a tunic or T, or to the back of a cape.

The Empress Kneeling before St. Martin. *Embroidered tablon* *Franco-Flemish, 1430-1440.*

Heraldic Designs

The most distinctive medieval pattern was the heraldic design. People who lived before the Middle Ages used geometric designs and designs from nature, and some even used symbols, but never before the Middle Ages was there such an elaborate system of designing and recording coats of arms and emblems which were used to identify people. The knights who painted symbols on their shields introduced the idea of heraldic designs, but soon kings, nobles, guildsmen and merchants adopted designs for themselves and their families; these became known as coats of arms. They chose bold colors and, often, pictures that had symbolic meanings. Knights chose pictures of lions, dragons and ferocious beasts to show what fierce warriors they were, and guildsmen chose symbols that represented their professions; a baker might choose a picture of a rolling pin, a carpenter a saw. Pictures and symbols were a good way to recognize people and their professions, particularly during the Middle Ages, when few people could read.

The knight painted his symbol on his shield because the shield was large and it was held in front of the knight's body, where it was easily seen. Coats of arms that were used to decorate tunics and dresses kept the traditional shield shape as a background.

TO MAKE A HERALDIC DESIGN

For the very simplest heraldic design, use a shield shape divided by geometric shapes and painted in two contrasting colors:

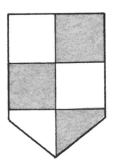

For a more interesting design add a picture or a symbol. Choose an animal, flower, bird, beast, mythological or made-up creature, your initial, a symbol of a medieval profession or even a medieval place (a castle, for instance). Use this symbol on a geometric background:

The art of heraldry became increasingly elaborate, and more symbols were added to the coat of arms. Although the shield shape decorated with a picture or symbol is sufficient to create a heraldic emblem for your costume, for absolute authenticity you can add:

The Crest, which sat above the shield shape:

The Motto, written below:

And "Supporters," animals or humans, which held up the shield at the sides:

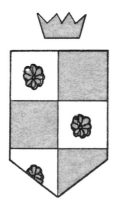

Two heraldic badges of recognition used as ornaments on horse trappings. Copper, silver, and enamel Italian, 15th century.

Quatrefoil with heraldry. Detail from an illuminated manuscript, The Belles Heures of Jean, Duke of Berry, *by Pol de Limbourg and his brothers Jean and Herman* French, ca. 1406-1409.

METHODS OF APPLYING DESIGN

Stenciling

In stenciling, color is applied to your fabric through a cutout design. Because the stencil can be used over and over, it is a good method to use if you want to repeat the same design many times. It is also useful if you want to use the same design to decorate different costumes—if you are costuming a noble and his family you can make a stencil of a simple heraldic emblem and repeat the image on each of their costumes.

In making a design to cut out for a stencil, remember that you will be cutting out a whole area; any design you have drawn within this area will be lost when you cut out the major shape:

To put a design in the middle of an area, cut out a stencil of the larger area and apply the design to your fabric. Then hand paint or appliqué the "inside" design onto the stenciled fabric:

Or make a second stencil for the inside design. Set this second stencil in place on the fabric over the larger design after that has dried. Use a darker color than the first to fill it in:

Make a separate stencil for each design you plan to use. This will permit you to use a different color for each design, and to print one shape on top of another. Any time you plan to overlap one design over part of another, use a darker-color paint to fill in the second shape. And be sure to wait for the first paint to dry.

You will need tracing paper, a pencil, a piece of cardboard, masking tape, large sheets of any inexpensive paper such as kraft paper (or even cut-open paper bags, but not newspapers), and an X-acto knife. An X-acto knife is a special cutting tool which can be purchased at any art supply store. It is very sharp, so be careful when you use it. If your costume is made of felt, use spray paint to fill in the stencil. For other fabrics use either spray paint or tempera paint applied with a brush. If you want to be able to send your costume to the cleaners or wash it, use textile or fabric paint to fill in the stencil. Spray and tempera paints will run when cleaned.

1. Draw your design on tracing paper.

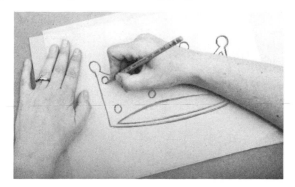

2. Make a CARBON TRANSFER to transfer the design on the tracing paper to the cardboard:

Hold your pencil so it is lying almost flat. Cover the back of the tracing paper with broad pencil marks—this will make the back of the tracing paper act like carbon paper. Turn the tracing paper over and tape it to the cardboard. Use a sharp pencil and trace around the outline of your design.

Remove the tracing paper.

3. Use the X-acto knife to cut out the design.

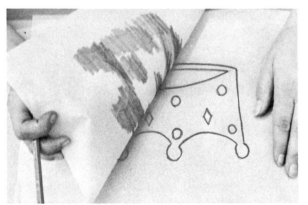
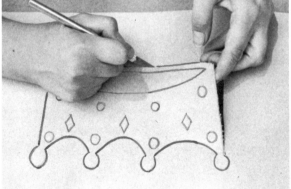

4. Prepare your fabric for printing: Make sure it is not wrinkled. Put large sheets of paper or old sheets down on a table and place the fabric on top of the paper. Make sure the fabric lies flat. If you are stenciling the pattern onto a tunic or T-shaped gown, insert several layers of the large sheets of paper between the front and the back of the gown so that the paint applied to the fabric doesn't soak through from one layer to the other.

5. Position the stencil and hold it in place.

6. Use spray paint or paint and brushes to fill in the design.

Wipe extra paint off the stencil as you work. Wait until the fabric is thoroughly dry before you stencil another pattern or apply any decoration to the painted areas.

Appliqué

In appliqué you use cutout pieces of fabric, scraps, ribbon and odds and ends to make a design. An appliquéd design combines different colors and textures, and appliquéing a picture is like painting with fabric. It is a particularly good technique to use for heraldic designs. Appliqué can also be used for tablons and borders, and it is very effective combined with another technique--you can hand paint or stencil a large shape and then outline it or decorate it with appliquéd designs.

You can use any fabric, but felt is the easiest to work with because the edges don't unravel when you cut out the pieces of the design. In addition to fabric you will need tracing paper, a pencil, cardboard, masking tape, scissors, straight pins, white glue, needle and thread, yarn and any ribbon or beads or other things you want to incorporate into the design.

1. Draw the design or designs on tracing paper.
2. Use the carbon transfer technique (see page 64) and transfer the design(s) to the piece of cardboard.
3. Cut out all the cardboard shapes.

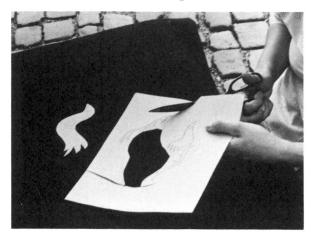

4. Place each cardboard shape on the piece of fabric you want to use for it and trace around it. Cut out all the fabric pieces for your design.
5. The tracing-paper drawing will act as your "master plan" so you can remember where each piece of fabric should be placed to make up the whole design. Pin all the pieces in place on your costume. If you are making a heraldic emblem it is easiest to pin and sew all the pieces to the shield shape first and then sew the shield shape to the costume.

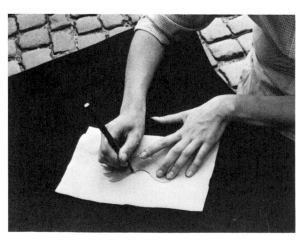

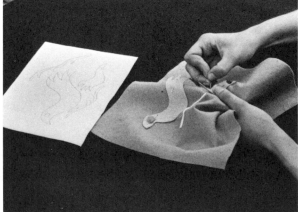

6. Use white glue for small shapes only.

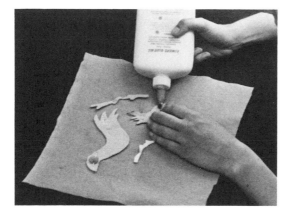

7. Sew the pieces of your design into place.

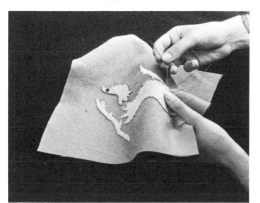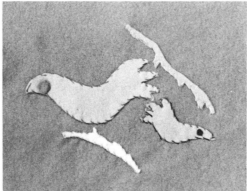

To add color and texture to the design you can sew the pieces to your costume with yarn and use a variety of decorative stitches.

RUNNING   *OVERCAST*   *CROSS*

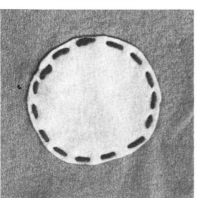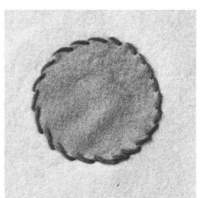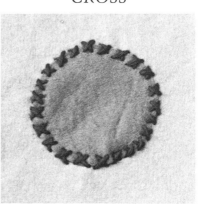

You can also "stuff" some of the appliquéd shapes to make them stand out and give your design extra dimension. Sew around ¾ of the shape. Stuff cotton, batting or small scraps of material into the shape and sew it closed.

Hand Painting

Painting on fabric is similar to painting on paper. The colors you choose, how thick or thin the paint is and the shape and size of your brushes all add variety to your picture. Hand painting your costume is a good process to use for tablons or picture stories, for emblems, for coloring a large area of your costume or dividing the costume into sections. You can also paint in details on stenciled or appliquéd designs.

Paint cannot be applied to sheer fabric. It will adhere to felt only if it is applied thickly, which makes it difficult to paint in a large design on a felt costume. It is easiest to use spray paint for filling in large areas on a felt costume, or, because paint takes easily to cotton, muslin and velvet, you can paint the designs on one of these fabrics and then sew the painted fabric onto your felt costume.

You will need tracing paper, a pencil, large sheets of paper, paint and brushes. If you want to be able to wash or dry clean your costume use textile or fabric paint. Otherwise, use tempera paint.

1. Draw the design on tracing paper. Use a carbon transfer (see page 64) and transfer the outline of the design to the fabric.

2. Prepare your fabric for painting: Make sure it is not wrinkled. Put large sheets of paper down on a table and place the fabric on top of the paper. Make sure the fabric lies flat. If you are painting a T or a tunic, insert several layers of the large sheets of paper between the front and the back of the costume so paint doesn't soak through from the front to the back of the costume.

3. Paint in the design.

ADORNMENTS

These are things which can be sewn onto your costume to give it a more medieval look:

BELLS

Bells not only were worn by court jesters, but were a popular accessory placed on belts and at the necklines and hemlines of nobles' clothing. If the color and grandness of a noble's clothing didn't catch your attention when he entered a room, then the tinkling of bells attached to his gown did.

Small silver- or gold-colored bells can be purchased at local sewing or novelty stores. Sew them onto your costumes or attach them to your belt.

BUTTONS

Buttons were not used to close clothes in the Middle Ages. These small round discs were used as decorations and sewn in straight rows down the fronts of gowns and from the elbows to the cuffs on sleeves. It seems odd that buttons were not used as fastenings. One possible explanation is that medieval people thought that because they allowed you to open and close your clothing so easily, buttons represented the "loose life." In any case, medieval T's were so roomy that they were easily slipped over the head and buttons were not really necessary.

The buttons you choose should be identical and made of wood or metal. Use them on costumes for kings, queens, nobles or merchants, sewn in straight rows down the front of the gown or on the sleeves.

FUR

We think of fur as a luxury and might mistakenly assume that it was worn only by nobles. Fur was a necessity in the Middle Ages. For one thing, houses were not heated, and they were cold and dark. Also, many laborers worked out of doors and they needed protection from the cold winter weather. Peasants as well as nobles used fur to line their clothing. But while the peasant used hides from beavers and badgers and other small animals he could easily trap, the noble demanded ermine and sable, which were rare and very expensive. The noble's fur had to be beautiful as well as warm; a favorite fur called "vair" was a combination of squirrel and ermine.

Real fur is obviously too expensive to use on your costume. Most sewing shops sell imitation or furlike material. Sometimes you can find a woolly fabric which looks like sheep or lamb, or even an old bathroom carpet can do the trick. Use the imitation fur to line a cape, or as a trim on a cape, tunic or gown. On a queen's or noblewoman's gown you can use a strip of fur to create a low waistline.

Directions for making a fur collar are given in the descriptions of costumes for the king and queen.

EMBROIDERED RIBBON

Instead of designing your own border you can buy embroidered or velvet ribbon at your sewing store to sew on as trim on your costume.

❖ACCESSORIES FOR YOUR COSTUME

PAPIER-MÂCHÉ

The instructions for many projects in this section will call for you to use "papier-mâché." Papier-mâché is a way of covering a surface with paper and glue to make the surface hard and solid. You build a frame of cardboard or chicken wire and cover it over with papier-mâché to form a completed shape.

To make papier-mâché you need a bowl, newspapers and a glue made from water and wallpaper paste. Wallpaper paste can be purchased at a hardware store.

1. Mix the glue. Start with one cup of wallpaper paste. Pour the paste into the bowl and add some water. Use about three times as much water as you do wallpaper paste. Mix it with your hand to get out the lumps. It will feel sticky. Keep adding water and mixing it in until the glue has the right consistency. When you are finished mixing, the wallpaper paste and water mixture should look like oatmeal.

2. Tear the sheets of newspaper into pieces or strips. *Always tear the newspaper, do not cut it.* Make the pieces and strips a sensible size in relation to the surface you are covering. To cover a small circle, use small pieces of newspaper; to cover a larger area, use large strips.

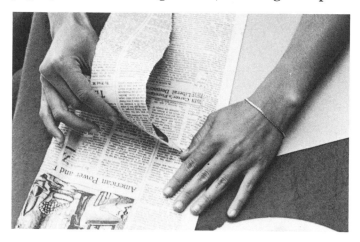

3. Spread the glue on the newspaper. Do not dunk the strips of newspaper into the bowl of glue, because you will end up with too much glue on the newspaper and it will be messy and hard to handle.

4. Apply the newspaper to the area you want to cover. To get a flat surface, overlap the pieces of newspaper at the edges as you apply them. Wipe off any excess glue.

5. Always wait until the papier-mâché is completely dry (about 24 hours) before you paint or decorate it.

Steel breastplate North German. 16th century.

BREASTPLATE AND BACKPLATE

To protect himself in battle the knight wore a metal breastplate and backplate. Often the breastplate was decorated with a heraldic emblem, which was made by applying extra strips of metal to the armor to form the outline of the design. This emblem was decorative, and the extra strips of metal strengthened the armor. But this decoration served the knight in another way, as well. The strips of metal formed ridges along the breastplate which caught his opponent's lance and prevented it from slipping off the breastplate and gouging the knight in the arm.

To make armor you apply papier-mâché to a chicken-wire form. You will need a large sheet of paper, pencil, scissors, 1½ yards of 36-inch-wide chicken wire, a wire cutter, masking tape, wallpaper paste, water, a bowl and newspapers for the papier-mâché, string, white glue, tempera paint and brushes, silver spray paint, and crystal-clear fixative. Crystal-clear fixative can be purchased at an art supply store.

1. Make a paper pattern for the breastplate. Since this piece of armor was shaped like a tunic, you can follow the instructions for making an ANGLED TUNIC which ends 10 inches below your waist or improvise a fancier design. Cut out the paper pattern. If you use the tunic pattern, make sure you cut the tunic across the top of the shoulders.
2. Tape the pattern to the chicken wire.

3. Use the wire cutter and cut around the pattern.

4. Remove the paper pattern. The backplate is the same shape as the breastplate so repeat steps 2 and 3 and cut out a second piece of chicken wire.

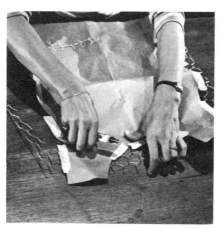 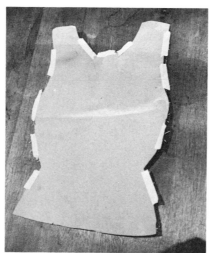

5. Cover the edges of the chicken wire with masking tape so you do not get scratched by the wire's rough edges.

6. Prepare the wallpaper paste mixture for papier-mâché. Cover the front and back of the breastplate with one layer of newspaper and glue. Cover the front and back of the backplate with one layer of newspaper and glue. The grid pattern of the chicken wire will show through, and the texture of the dry papier-mâché over the wire will give you a metallike effect.

7. After you have covered both pieces of chicken wire, place them on a drop cloth or newspaper to let them dry. Allow the papier-mâché to dry for a couple of hours, then, while they are still damp, mold each piece to give it a slightly rounded shape. Gently fold the edges of each side toward each other. Do this several times before the papier-mâché is dry.

8. In 24 hours, when the papier-mâché is completely dry, draw a heraldic design on the breastplate in pencil.

9. Use white glue and outline the design in string or braid.

10. Paint in the design and background color. When the paint is dry, spray the front of the breastplate with crystal-clear fixative to give it a shiny surface. Spray the back of the breastplate and the entire backplate with silver spray paint.

11. Use the point of a scissors and make a hole in the middle of the top of each shoulder, on both sides of the neckline of the breastplate and the backplate.
12. Tie a piece of string or cord to each shoulder through these holes.

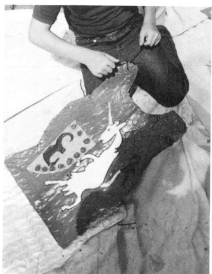

13. For extra support, attach ties in the same way at both sides of the armor.
14. Have someone help you tie the breastplate and the backplate together at your shoulders and your sides.

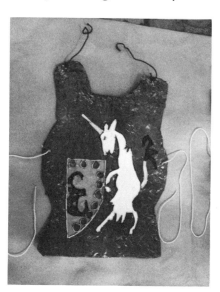

SWORD

Legend tells us that Arthur became King of England because he was able to dislodge a sword from a stone. The sword was not only a powerful weapon, it was an important symbol to the knight. A squire knelt before his king, and with a tap on the shoulders from the blade of the king's sword he was dubbed a knight. With the same reverence as those who place their hands on the Bible to "swear to God," the knight clasped his hands on the handle of his sword to pledge an undying vow. In fact, since swords resembled the shape of a cross, the vow was sacred as well as political.

The knight's sword was over three feet long. It had a knob at the top called a pommel, and the handle was called a hilt.

You will need a piece of heavy cardboard, a pencil, X-acto knife, string, white glue, black or brown paint and a brush and silver spray paint.

1. Use these pictures as models to design a sword and draw it on the cardboard.
2. Use the X-acto knife to cut out the sword. If the cardboard is not thick enough, place the cutout pattern on another piece of cardboard, trace around it and cut out a second sword. Glue the two together.
3. To give the handle a different texture from the blade of the sword, wrap string around the pommel and the hilt and glue it in place.
4. Paint the string-covered handle brown or black.
5. Spray paint the blade silver.

Sword with silver pommel
Italian, 15th century.

SHIELD

The knight on horseback held a triangular shield which covered the entire left side of his body. The shield was about five feet long and was curved in toward his body. It seems like a good idea to "shield" as much of the knight's body as possible, but because of its size the shield sometimes got in the knight's way, and of course it added extra weight to his already heavy costume. Nevertheless, the shield offered good protection to the knight who became expert at manipulating it. Wooden shields covered with leather were used by many ancient civilizations, but it was not until the Middle Ages that they took on this large, kitelike shape.

Notice the shield of the knight on horseback. Ivory chessman
Probably English, ca. 1370.

You will need cardboard, a pencil, scissors, paint and brushes, crystal-clear fixative, masking tape and silver spray paint.

1. Use these pictures as models and design and draw a shield on cardboard.
2. Cut out the shield.
3. Draw a heraldic design on the front of the shield and paint it in. Cover the whole front with paint.
4. Spray the dry, painted front of the shield with crystal-clear fixative.
5. Attach a loop to the back so you can hold the shield in front of your body: Use a strip of cardboard 2 inches wide and 12 inches long. Measure 2 inches in at the top of the strip and 2 inches in at the bottom. Fold each of these 2-inch tabs out to make an edge for taping. Position the loop horizontally and tape it to the back of the shield, as shown in the photograph.
6. Spray paint the back of the shield silver.

Jewelry

Unlike other accessories which are popular and then out of fashion, jewelry has always remained popular. Jewelry is attractive, expensive, and a symbol that the wearer is wealthy. It is also an investment, and while the value of money varies from country to country, jewelry is internationally recognized as valuable. Jewelry can be bartered or traded and used instead of money to buy food and clothing. In the Middle Ages the value of jewelry took on additional significance. While it was the law in many provinces that only her son could inherit a mother's land, serfs and money, jewelry could be left to her daughter. So by investing in jewels a medieval mother insured her daughter's inheritance.

Only noble men and women wore jewelry. Pearls and rubies were the rarest jewels and so they were the most popular. Some of the gems used in medieval jewelry were not very rare, but they were valued for their "magical powers." The toadstone, for example, changed color. It was believed that the toadstone changed color when it was near poison, and it protected the wearer by alerting him to danger.

Sleeves on medieval gowns were long and there was not much interest in bracelets; but rings, medallions, brooches and belt buckles were all fashionable items of medieval jewelry.

Notice the jewelry on both men and women. Detail from a tapestry, Noblemen and Noblewomen on a Background of Rosebushes *Franco-Flemish, 1435-1440.*

BROOCH

A brooch can be used to fasten a cape or as a hat ornament. Gather a collection of "found jewels," such as sequins, buttons, rhinestones, old earrings, to be used to decorate the brooch. You will also need a pencil, cardboard, scissors, paint, a paint brush, white glue and a flat-backed jewelry pin (not a safety pin). This type of pin can be purchased at any jewelry or craft supply store.

1. Draw a circle or a square 3 inches wide on cardboard and cut it out.
2. Paint the front, back and sides of the cardboard circle or square any solid color. You can use gold or silver spray paint to simulate the look of metal.
3. Glue on your jewels. You can place them randomly or in a geometric design.
4. When the jewels on the front are completely set, glue the pin to the back of the brooch.

BELT BUCKLE

An ornamented belt buckle can be used with a belt you already have or attached to a piece of leather. You will need a ruler, cardboard, a pencil, scissors, paint, a paint brush, white glue and a collection of "found jewels."

1. Measure the width of your belt or the strip of leather you intend to use as a belt.
2. Draw a circle one inch wider than your belt on the cardboard and cut it out.
3. Paint the front, back and sides of the circle any solid color. You can use gold or silver spray paint to simulate the look of metal.
4. Glue on your jewels.
5. When the jewels on the front are completely set, attach a loop to the back of the buckle: Use a strip of cardboard ½ inch long and the width of the circle. Measure ¼ inch in at each end of the strip. Fold these two ¼-inch tabs in toward the middle of the strip. Fold them back for taping. Tape the loop to the back of the buckle.
6. Slip the belt through the loop on the buckle. To wear, fasten the belt and slide the buckle around to the front.

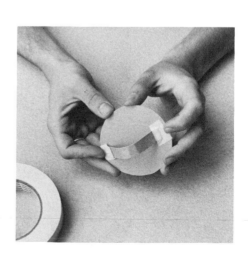

MEDALLION

For the medallion you will need small, thin pieces of colored glass broken into various geometric shapes. This colored glass is used in stained-glass work and is available at craft supply stores. You will also need cardboard, a pencil, scissors, paint, a paint brush and white glue. Your medallion will look most authentic if it is strung from a real chain. Perhaps you have a chain from an old necklace that you can use; or you can purchase an inexpensive jewelry chain at a local store. If not, buy 18 inches of thin metal chain from a hardware store.

1. Draw a circle 4 inches wide on the cardboard and cut it out.
2. Use a hole punch or the point of your scissors to make a hole near the top edge of the circle.
3. Paint the back and the edges of the circle any solid color.
4. On the front of the medallion paint a picture or a design.
5. Use the pieces of colored glass to make a mosaic out of the painted design and give it a medieval look. Randomly glue the pieces of glass over the design. Do not cover the hole you punched.
6. String the chain through the hole.

Hats

With no other clue you can identify every medieval character by his hat: A knight wears a helmet, a king wears a crown, and who else but the court jester would wear a floppy hat with ears and bells?

CROWN

The crown is a symbol of royalty. It is passed down from generation to generation and worn by the king, as a sign that he is the ruler of a country. If a medieval king lost a war or his country was invaded, he would give his crown to the victor, as a symbol that this conqueror now ruled his kingdom.

Crown. Detail from an illuminated manuscript, The Belles Heures of Jean, Duke of Berry, *by Pol de Limbourg and his brothers Jean and Herman* French, ca. 1406-1409.

You will need a tape measure, a piece of cardboard, tracing paper, pencil, scissors, masking tape, string, white glue, gold spray paint and "found jewels."

1. Have someone help you and measure around your head. You will need a piece of cardboard at least 5 inches high and 1 inch longer than the length you have just measured.
2. Use a piece of tracing paper with the same dimensions as the cardboard to design your crown.
The most common crown was pointed. But other designs were popular too:

When you plan out the pattern for your crown on the tracing paper, remember that your drawing is flat, but the crown will be circular. When you cut out the crown and tape it to form a circle that sits on top of your head, what you have drawn on the left-hand side of the paper will be joined to what you have drawn on the right-hand side.
3. Make a carbon transfer (page 64) and transfer the tracing-paper design to the cardboard.
4. Cut out the crown.

5. Draw simple geometric shapes on the crown and outline them with string. Glue on the string. Emphasize the shape of the crown by outlining it in string too.

6. Wrap the crown into a circle and join the ends with masking tape.

7. Spray paint the entire crown, inside and out, with gold spray paint.

8. After the paint has dried, glue on your jewels.

Nobleman wearing a hat. Detail from a tapestry, Honor and Her Children *French, early 15th century.*

MAN'S HAT

Hats were worn indoors as well as out. Toward the end of the Middle Ages hats worn by nobles were large and outlandish and so heavy and unwieldy that they had to be pinned in place on the noble's head. This hat can be worn by noblemen and merchants and pinned in place to the hair with a jeweled brooch or feather.

You will need a tape measure, wire, wire cutters, masking tape, foam rubber, scissors, fabric and needle and thread. For the fabric use felt, velvet or any material which has some body but is not stiff. The hat will be made up of 2 parts: the brim, and the crown, or top of the hat. You can paint a design on the fabric before you use it to make the crown.

1. To make the brim of the hat: Have someone measure around your head. Measure and cut a piece of wire 2 inches longer than the length you have just measured. This is the *length of the wire.*

2. Wrap the piece of wire into a circle and twist the ends of the wire around each other just enough to keep them together. Secure them with masking tape.

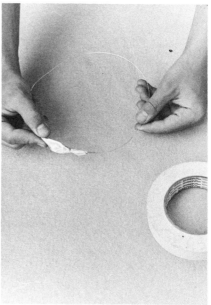

3. Use strips of foam rubber about 1 inch thick to pad the wire. Twist the foam rubber around the wire and wrap pieces of masking tape around the circle to hold the foam rubber in place.

4. To cover the foam rubber roll, measure the thickness of the padded circle. You will need a piece of fabric ½ inch wider than this and 1 inch longer than the length of the wire. Use the same fabric you will use to make the crown of the hat or a piece of contrasting velvet or fur.

5. Sew the fabric around the foam rubber.

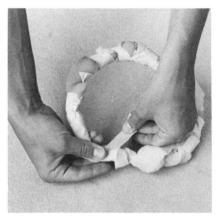 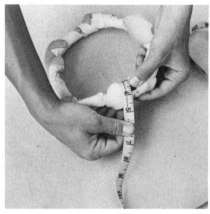 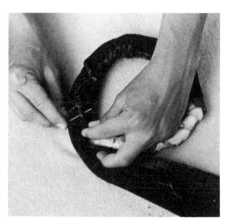

6. To make the crown of the hat: Use a piece of fabric half the length of the wire and 30 inches long. Fold the material in half from top to bottom. (Each side should measure 15 inches.) Sew the front and the back together at each of the sides.

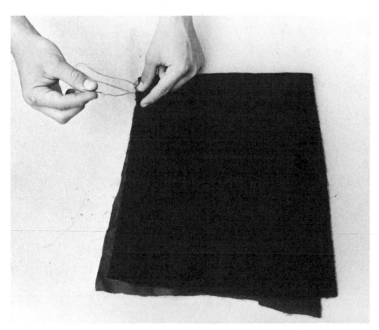

7. Sew the open, bottom edge of the fabric to the inside of the foam rubber roll.

8. Arrange the material of the crown of the hat so that it falls to the side. Hold the crown in place with a pin, brooch or feather pinned to the folds.

HOOD

The hood is worn by peddlers, peasants, minstrels and monks; it is the simplest head covering, worn by the simplest characters.

You will need a piece of material 10 inches wide by 30 inches long, a needle and thread, scissors and 2 feet of cord. Use felt, burlap or any rough-textured fabric.

1. Fold the material in half from top to bottom to make a rectangle 10 inches wide by 15 inches long.

2. Sew the two layers of the folded material together at the left-hand side.

3. Try the hood on. Have someone help you and use a hole punch or the point of a scissors to make a hole in each side of the material underneath your chin.

4. Cut the cord in half. Tie each piece of cord to one of the holes.

5. To wear, tie the two pieces of cord under your chin.

HELMET

The face is a vulnerable area for the soldier. Some soldiers covered only the tops of their heads, but the medieval knight was willing to have his vision impaired and breathing made difficult in order to cover and protect his entire face. The helmet had several different shapes, but one of the most popular was the basinet, which had a visor which could be lifted when the knight was not in battle.

The helmet is made of two parts: a papier-mâché crown (top of the helmet) and a cardboard visor. You will need wallpaper paste, water, a bowl and newspapers for the papier-mâché. You will also need a tape measure, cardboard, scissors, masking tape, pencil, a ruler, another piece of cardboard 7½ inches long by 17 inches wide, 2 paper fasteners and silver spray paint.

Steel helmet Italian, early 16th century.

1. To make the crown: Have someone help you and measure around your head, just above your eyebrows.
2. You will need a strip of cardboard 2 inches wide and 1 inch longer than the length you have just measured. Make the strip of cardboard into a circle and join the ends with masking tape.
3. Cut four strips of cardboard which are each 1 inch wide and 14 inches long.

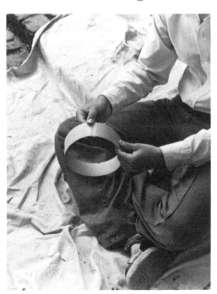

4. Use these cardboard strips to cross the top of the circle and form the arch of the helmet: Try on the cardboard circle. Have someone help. Take one of the cardboard strips and tape it to the middle of the front of the circle.
5. Arch the cardboard strip over your head and tape the other end to the middle of the back of the circle. Cut off any excess cardboard.

 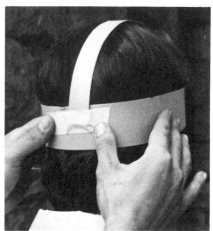

6. Take off the circle; use the three other cardboard strips to create more arcs that cross the first one at the center.
7. Tape the overlapping strips of cardboard together at the center.
8. Prepare the wallpaper paste mixture for papier-mâché. Apply three layers of papier-mâché to the outside of the crown. (Do not papier-mâché the inside.)

9. While the crown is drying, cut out the visor: Fold the 7½-inch-by-17-inch piece of cardboard in half from left to right so that you have a rectangle 7½ inches long and 8½ inches wide. The fold in the cardboard is on the left-hand side.

10. This drawing is a small, or scale, version of the pattern for the visor. Use a ruler and measure and mark the distances and lines shown on this drawing onto the cardboard. The result will be a full-size drawing of the visor on the cardboard. Although it will be larger, the shape on the cardboard should match the shape in the pattern drawing. The black square in the middle of the pattern is an eyehole. Mark it onto your cardboard.

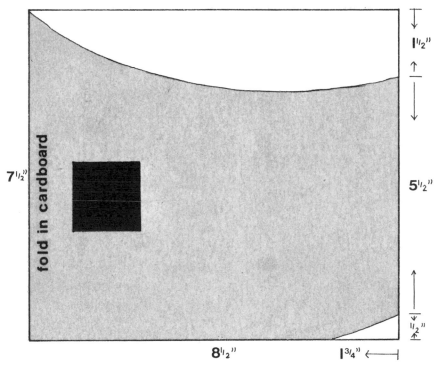

11. Cut out the visor. Then cut out the eyeholes.

12. Wait 24 hours until the crown is completely dry to attach the visor to the crown: Use the point of a scissors to make a hole in the upper right-hand corner and one in the upper left-hand corner of the unfolded visor.

13. Use the point of a scissors to make a hole in the headband of the crown.

14. Put a paper fastener through the hole on the left-hand side of the visor and the hole on the headband of the crown to attach the two pieces.

15. Make another hole on the headband, opposite the first, with the point of the scissors. Put a paper fastener through the hole on the right-hand side of the visor and this hole on the headband of the crown. The paper fasteners will allow you to lift the visor and wear it perched on your helmet.

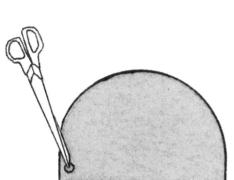
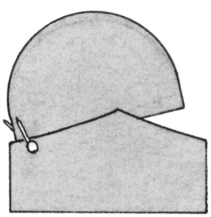
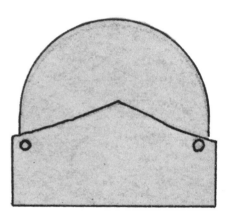

16. Spray paint the entire helmet silver. For a tournament helmet you can attach a feather through the top of the crown.

WOMAN'S HEADDRESS

This winged headdress was a popular medieval creation worn by noblewomen.

The headdress will be made in two parts: a papier-mâché skullcap and cardboard "wings" which sit on top of the cap. You will need wallpaper paste, water, a bowl and newspapers for the papier-mâché. You will also need a Styrofoam head form (used for wigs), which can be purchased at most department or beauty stores, Vaseline, a flat knife, a stapler, paper towels, scissors, a pencil, two pieces of cardboard each measuring 7½ inches long by 6½ inches wide, a ruler, paint and brushes, white glue and ribbon, braid or cord.

1. To make the skullcap: Cover the top and the entire forehead of the Styrofoam head with Vaseline. This layer of Vaseline between the head and the papier-mâché will make it easy to remove the cap when it is dry.

2. Prepare the wallpaper paste mixture for papier-mâché. Cover the top of the head and the forehead with three layers of papier-mâché.

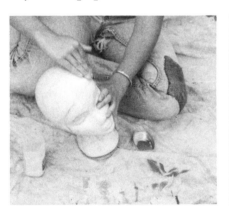  

3. Wait at least 24 hours until the cap is completely dry. Insert a flat knife along the rim of the cap to loosen it from the head form. This will probably loosen the cap enough for it to be completely and easily removed from the model. If the cap does not slip right off, use an X-acto knife and cut the cap in half, remove the two halves and staple them together. Wipe out the inside of the skullcap with a paper towel to remove the excess Vaseline.

4. Cut out a small arc, about 1 inch deep, along the front of the cap.

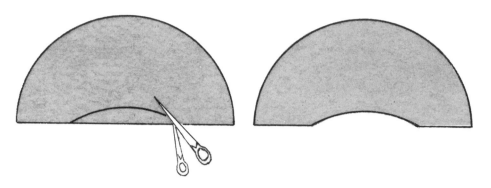

5. To make the wings: Use a ruler and measure and mark the distances and lines shown on this scale drawing on each piece of cardboard. Each wing will be full size. Although they will be larger, the shapes on the cardboard should match the shape in the drawing.

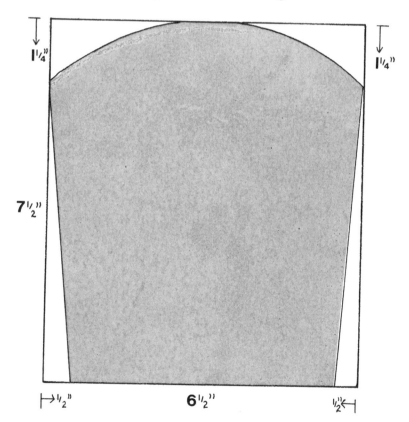

6. Cut out the cardboard wings.

7. Position each of the pieces of cardboard at an opposite side of the skullcap and staple them in place.

8. Papier-mâché the wings. If you had to cut the skullcap to remove it from the model, then papier-mâché the entire skullcap as well to cover over the staples and the seam.

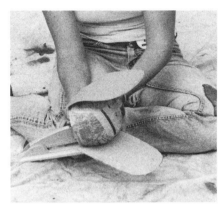 

9. When the papier-mâché is dry, paint the headdress one color.

10. Use ribbon, braid or cord to decorate the wings.

11. To wear, use bobby pins to pin the hat in place to your hair.

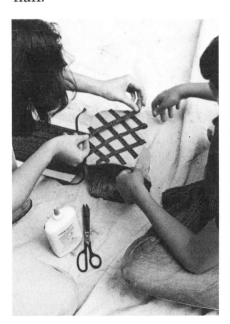 

Bishop's miter. Silver brocade with gold and coral decorations Austrian, 13th century.

MITER

The miter was designed in the Middle Ages as a special hat to be worn by the bishop.

You will need two pieces of white oak tag, each 12 inches square. (You can use regular cardboard and paint the hat white.) You will also need a pencil, a ruler, scissors, transparent tape, white glue and 5 feet of 1- to 2-inch-wide embroidered ribbon.

1. The front and the back of the miter are the same shape. Use a ruler to measure and mark off the distances and lines shown in this scale drawing of the miter on each of the two pieces of oak tag. The drawings on the oak tag will be full-size patterns for the miter. Although they will be larger, the shapes on the oak tag should match the shape in the drawing.

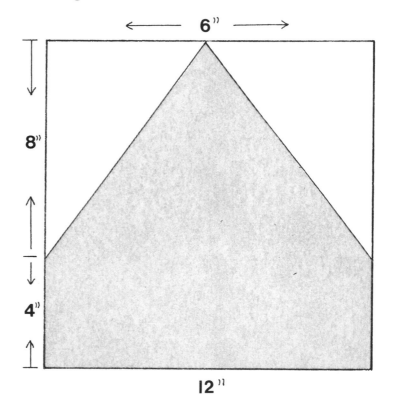

2. Cut out the two pieces.

3. Measure and mark a ½-inch strip on the short sides of each of the pieces of oak tag.

4. Fold each of these strips in toward the middle and let them stand up so that they each form an L.

5. Turn over one piece of oak tag and place it on top of the other. Let the folded strips on the top piece of oak tag overlap the strips on the bottom piece. These strips form the narrow sides of the hat.

6. Tape the hat together at the sides.

7. Glue ribbon around the base of the miter and cut a piece to be attached down the middle of the front of the hat. Cut the leftover ribbon in half. Tape the two pieces to the inside of the back of the miter so they hang down from the base of the hat.

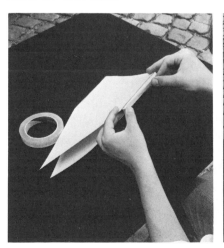  

Hennin. Detail from a tapestry,
Judith and Holofernes *Flemish.*
15th century.

HENNIN

The word hennin has no real meaning. We think it was an insult that was shouted at noblewomen who wore tall, cylindrical hats. The name stuck, and despite the insults, the "hennin" became the most popular hat worn in the Middle Ages. Noblewomen tried to outdo each other, each attempting to balance a larger and more outrageous cone-shaped hat on her head. As the fashion to make these hats larger and larger continued, castle doorways had to be enlarged to accommodate the towering creations.

You will need a piece of oak tag or thin cardboard 22 inches long and 28 inches wide, a piece of felt the same size, a pencil, a ruler, scissors, masking tape, a stapler and 2 feet of ribbon. You will also need a streamer of chiffon, or any lightweight material to attach to the top of the hennin.

1. This drawing is a small version of the hennin pattern. Measure and mark the distances and lines indicated on this drawing on the piece of cardboard. You will have a full-size drawing of the hennin on the cardboard. Although it will be larger, the shape on the cardboard should match the shape in the pattern.

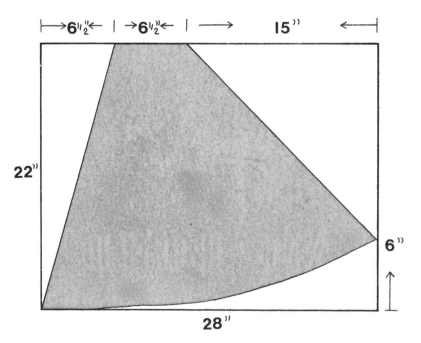

2. Cut out the cardboard.

3. Wrap the cardboard into a cone and have someone help fit it to your head. The edges of the cardboard will overlap.

4. Tape down the overlapping seam.

5. Trim any extra cardboard at the bottom of the hat so the base line is even.

6. Measure and mark the same pattern onto the felt. Cut it out.

7. Staple the felt around the cardboard. The edges of the felt will overlap, and again, you will probaly need to trim the material around the base of the hat.

8. Use the point of the scissors to make two holes, opposite each other, along the base of the hat.
9. Cut the ribbon in half and tie one piece to each of the holes.

10. Staple the streamer of material to the top of the hat. You can also add a border of ribbon around the base or randomly glue "jewels" to the hennin.
11. To wear, balance the hennin on your head and tie a bow underneath your chin.

This stained glass window (German, ca. 1480–1490) shows a peasant woman preparing a meal, two noble couples, and a court jester. Notice the short costume and pointed shoes of the young nobleman on the right, the jester's cap and bells, and that the peasant's head is covered. The Metropolitan Museum of Art, Samuel P. Avery Memorial Fund, 11.120.2

Detail from a tapestry, **Hector and Andromache,** *from the Workshop of Pasquier Grenier (Franco-Flemish, 1472–1474). Hector is being helped into his armor. Notice the helmet of the armored man on horseback, the headdresses and necklaces worn by the noblewomen, and the rich patterns of the costumes.*

The Metropolitan Museum of Art, Fletcher Fund, 39.74

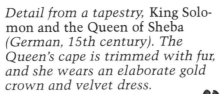

Detail from a tapestry, King Solomon and the Queen of Sheba *(German, 15th century). The Queen's cape is trimmed with fur, and she wears an elaborate gold crown and velvet dress.*

The Metropolitan Museum of Art, The Cloisters Collection, 1971.43

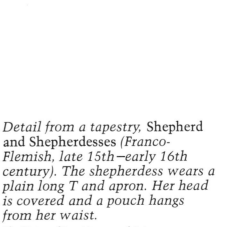

Detail from a tapestry, Shepherd and Shepherdesses *(Franco-Flemish, late 15th—early 16th century). The shepherdess wears a plain long T and apron. Her head is covered and a pouch hangs from her waist.*

The Metropolitan Museum of Art, Gift of George Blumenthal, 41.100.196

Details from an illuminated manuscript, The Belles Heures of Jean, Duke of Berry, *by Pol de Limbourg and his brothers Jean and Herman (French, ca. 1406–1409).*

Notice the peasant's costume is short so it doesn't interfere with his planting. His head is covered and he uses his tunic as a pouch.

Houses were cold and drafty in the Middle Ages. This elderly townsman warming his hands by the fire wears a hood and fur hat for extra warmth.

Another peasant in a short T. He is barefoot but his head is covered by a brimmed straw hat to protect him from the sun.

A Rustic Concert. *Underside of a marriage salver, tempera on wood, from the Workshop of Lorenzo di Niccolò (Italian, ca. 1392–1411). The women's dresses have wide scalloped sleeves. The simply dressed men, probably peasants, wear hoods. Notice the coats of arms of the bride's and groom's families at the top of the painting.*

King Solomon and the Queen of Sheba. *Painting in tempera on wood, from the Workshop of Sano di Pietro (Italian, 15th century). Simply dressed townspeople herald the arrival of the Queen of Sheba. Their clothes are dark and plain, with only an occasional belt and collar.*

The Metropolitan Museum of Art, Rogers Fund, 14.44

Noblemen and Noblewomen on a Background of Rosebushes. *Tapestry (Franco-Flemish, 1435–1440). The men wear short, fur-trimmed T's and large, floppy hats. The women wear heavily brocaded gowns and large, winglike headdresses. Both wear medallions.*

The Metropolitan Museum of Art, Rogers Fund, 09.137.3

Detail from one of The Nine Heroes Tapestries, *probably by Nicholas Bataille (French, ca. 1385). The fleur-de-lis is used as a heraldic symbol on the flags which fly from the turrets of the castle walls. This design is repeated in the crowns of the two queens.*

CIRCLET

The circlet is a simple head covering which can be worn by noblewomen or young maidens.

You will need a tape measure, cardboard, scissors, pencil, masking tape, felt, white glue, paint and a brush, "found jewels" and an 18-inch-square piece of fabric. Choose chiffon, or any other light, airy material.

1. Have someone help you and measure around your head. You will need a piece of cardboard 1 inch wide and the length you have just measured.
2. Wrap the strip of cardboard into a circle so that the ends just overlap, and join the ends with masking tape.
3. Cut two strips of felt, each 1 inch wide and the same length as the cardboard. Glue one strip to the inside and the other to the outside of the circle.
4. Paint the top edge of the circle.
5. Decorate the circle with "found jewels."
6. To wear the circlet, drape the square piece of material over your head and place the circlet over it.

COURT JESTER'S CAP

Just as his tunic was an exaggeration of the clothes worn by everyday people, the jester's cap was an extravagant version of the hood.

You will need two pieces of material, one for the back of the hat and one for the front. Use two different-colored pieces of felt, each 18 inches long and 14 inches wide. You will also need a pencil, a ruler, scissors, a salad plate, yarn, yarn needle and three small metal bells.

1. Measure and cut each of the two pieces of felt separately. Fold each of the pieces of felt in half from left to right. You will have two rectangles, 18 inches long and 7 inches wide, with the fold in the material on the left-hand side.
2. Use a ruler and measure and mark the distances and lines shown in this scale drawing of the pattern for the jester's hat on each piece of felt. The shapes on the felt will be larger, but should match the shape in the pattern drawing.

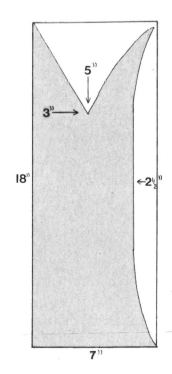

3. Cut out the two pieces. Unfold each piece of material.
4. Choose one piece to be the front of the hat. To cut an opening for your face: Use a salad plate or any flat, circular object which is 7 to 8 inches in diameter. Place the plate in the middle of the felt.
5. Trace around the plate.
6. Cut out the circle.

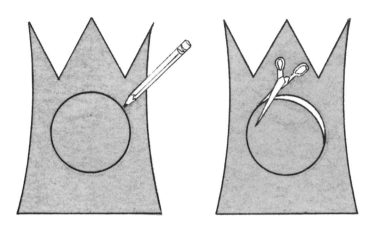

7. Use brightly colored yarn to sew the front and the back of the hat together. Leave the bottom edge free.
8. Sew the bells to the points of the cap.

ROBIN HOOD HAT

You will need two pieces of green felt, each 16 inches long and 8 inches high, a pencil, a ruler, scissors and needle and thread.

1. The front and the back of the hat are the same shape. This drawing is a small version of the pattern for the Robin Hood hat. Use a ruler and measure and mark the distances and lines shown on this drawing on each piece of felt. Although the shapes on the felt will be larger, they should match the shape in the drawing.

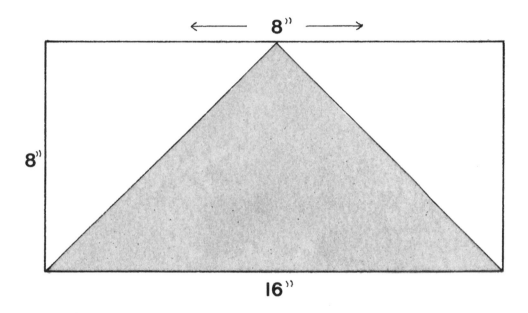

2. Cut out the two pieces.
3. Place one of the triangular pieces directly on top of the other, with all edges lining up.
4. Sew the two pieces together along both of the shorter sides. Leave the 16-inch bases free.
5. Fold up the brim of the hat. You can attach a feather.

SHOES

When a medieval couple was married, the father of the bride gave one of her shoes to the groom as a symbol that his daughter and all of her possessions now belonged to this man.

Shoes were a status symbol in the Middle Ages, and just as hats grew taller and taller, medieval shoes grew longer and longer. The basic shoe was made of leather or fabric and was soft and pliable. As the length of a man's shoe became equated with his wealth, the pointed toes on his shoes became so exaggerated that they had to be stuffed, or tied around a man's shins to keep him from falling over his own feet.

The shoe should be worn with the court jester, minstrel, noble, Robin Hood, peasant, or any costume where your feet show. You will need felt, a pencil, scissors, yarn and a

Leather and silver drinking cup
in the shape of a shoe
German. 16th century.

yarn needle. For a minstrel or court jester you can use two different-colored felts and make the shoes parti-colored, or make a different-colored shoe for each foot. You will also need one of your socks as a model for the shoe.

1. Place the sock on the felt and trace around the foot area, leaving a 1-inch border all around. You can make the toe as long or as pointed as you want.
2. The shoe is ankle height. Make a slightly curved line ending the shoe pattern just above the heel.

3. Cut out the pattern.
4. Place the cutout pattern on another piece of felt and trace around it. Repeat this twice more, so you have four patterns in all. Cut them out.
5. Use yarn to sew two pieces of the felt together. Sew around the whole shoe, but leave the curved line above the heel free.

6. Sew the remaining two pieces of felt together.

To make the points of the shoe stand up, stuff each toe with cotton or small pieces of material.

To tie the points of your shoes to your shins, sew a long piece of yarn or cord to the toe of each shoe. Try the shoes on, tie the cord around your leg (just beneath your knees), and cut off any extra cord.

POUCHES

Medieval gowns did not have pockets. People tied their possessions in the ends of their sleeves, or carried pouches tied around their waists. These small bags hung from the belts of both men and women. They contained coins, and perhaps a mirror or an extra hat pin, and usually held a piece of bread to be offered to a beggar.

The pouch can be round or square. If it is to be worn by a noble or a merchant, use a piece of velvet or satin, or decorate a piece of felt. A peasant's pouch should be made from plain, dark felt or burlap.

ROUND POUCH

You will need a 16-inch-square piece of material, a tape measure, a pencil, scissors, and a piece of cord or a thin leather strip 6 feet long.

Man with a pouch. Detail fom a tapestry, The Seven Sacraments, *from the Workshop of Pasquier Grenier* Franco-Flemish. ca. 1475.

1. Make a CIRCLE (with no central hole) out of the fabric. (The width of the circle is 8 inches.)
2. Cut ½-inch-long slits 1 inch apart around the edge of the circle. Use the photograph as a guide and make sure you do not cut through the edge of the material.
3. Weave the piece of cord in and out through the slits.
4. Gather the material on the cord.

  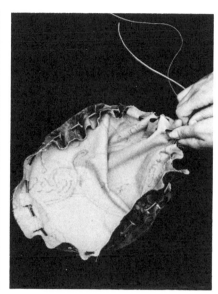

SQUARE POUCH

Use a piece of material 12 inches long and 6 inches wide. You will also need scissors, needle and thread and a piece of cord or thin strip of leather 2 feet long.

1. Cut ½-inch-long slits 1 inch apart along the top and the bottom of the material. Use the photograph as a guide and make sure you do not cut through the edge of the material.
2. Fold the material in half from bottom to top so you have a 6-inch square.
3. Sew the material together at the sides.
4. Weave the piece of cord in and out through the slits around the top of the bag.

Tie the pouch to your belt.

WANDS AND SCEPTERS

The scorcerer's wand was an important tool which helped him perform his magic. The king's wand, called a scepter, did not have powers of its own, but along with the crown it was a symbol of power, a sign that the king ruled over his country. Not to be outdone by the king, the bishop carried a crosier. This was a tall staff and it represented the bishop's power to lead the people. The wand carried by the court jester, on the other hand, did not stand for power or magic, but it did symbolize the court jester's job. The jester carried a wand known as a "fool's head," which was fashioned with a miniature sculpture of himself on top.

KING'S SCEPTER

You will need a ¼-inch dowel which is 18 inches long. (A dowel is a rounded stick, and you can buy them at hardware, lumber and most craft supply stores.) You will also need a Styrofoam ball 2 to 3 inches wide, scissors, wallpaper paste, water, newspapers and a bowl for papier-mâché, white glue, string, gold spray paint and "found jewels."

1. Use the point of the scissors to make a small hole about 1 inch deep in the Styrofoam ball.
2. Stick the dowel into this hole and push the dowel far enough into the ball so that it is held securely.

3. Prepare the wallpaper paste mixture for papier-mâché. Cover the entire Styrofoam ball with one layer of papier-mâché.

4. When the papier-mâché is dry, glue geometric string designs around the ball.
5. Spray paint the entire scepter.
6. Glue jewels around the ball.

SORCERER'S WAND

You will need a pencil, cardboard, scissors, white glue, a ¼-inch dowel which is 18 inches long and gold or silver spray paint.

1. Draw a large five-pointed star on the cardboard and cut it out.
2. Place the cutout star on another piece of cardboard, trace around it and cut out a second star.
3. Glue the edges of the stars together around the top and two side points. Leave the two bottom points of the star free.
4. The unglued bottom points of the star make an opening for the dowel. Slip the dowel in between the two stars.
5. Spray paint the entire wand.

BISHOP'S CROSIER

The top of the crosier is a curled shape decorated with jewels. You will need a Styrofoam "candy cane," ½ inch thick and 12 inches long, for the spiral, and a ½-inch dowel which is 4 feet long. The candy-cane shapes are sold at craft supply stores or stores specializing in Christmas decorations. If you cannot get a Styrofoam cane, you can fashion the curl out of wire and pad it with foam rubber, as shown in the instructions for making the brim of the man's hat. You will also need masking tape, wallpaper paste, water, newspapers and a bowl for papier-mâché, gold spray paint, white glue and "found jewels."

1. Hold the Styrofoam candy cane (or your improvised wire version) vertically, and tape it to the top of the dowel.
2. Prepare the wallpaper paste mixture for papier-mâché. Apply one layer of papier-mâché to entire staff to give it a uniform texture.
3. When the papier-mâché is dry, spray paint the staff.
4. Glue jewels around the curl.

Crozier head. Silver gilt and enamel Italian. 1457.

FOOL'S HEAD

You will need a Styrofoam ball 3 inches in diameter, scissors, a ¼-inch dowel which is 18 inches long, wallpaper paste, water, newspapers and a bowl for papier-mâché, paint and brushes and felt.

1. Use the point of the scissors to make a small hole in the Styrofoam ball.
2. Stick the dowel into this hole and push the dowel far enough into the ball so that it is held securely.
3. Prepare the wallpaper paste mixture for papier-mâché. Cover the entire ball with one layer of papier-mâché. Make the jester's face by sculpting it out of pieces of newspaper, held in place by the wallpaper paste glue. Crumple small pieces of newspaper into balls for the nose and eyes, and twist strips of newspaper to form the chin, mouth and eyebrows.
4. When the papier-mâché is dry, paint the jester's face.
5. Use the same color felt you used for your jester's hat to make a hat for the fool's head.

USES FOR MEDIEVAL COSTUMES

Maybe you first looked at this book because you are going to be in a play about the Middle Ages and you want to know how to make your costume. Perhaps you are dressing up for a costume party or Halloween and want to get some ideas, or maybe you are learning about the Middle Ages and want to know how people lived and dressed. Now that you know more about medieval times you can find many uses for the costumes described in this book.

You can write a skit based on a medieval legend, like the story of the Knights of the Round Table, or on a historical event, like the Crusades, or you can make up a story of everyday life in a castle or village. If you are going to be in a pageant or parade, you can suggest that the theme of the pageant be the Middle Ages and that everyone choose to portray a different medieval character. Or you can stage a medieval festival.

All of the photographs in this book were taken at the Medieval Festival which is held at The Cloisters every summer. The Cloisters is a medieval building which is part of The Metropolitan Museum of Art in New York City. As you can see in the backgrounds of the photographs, all the sidewalks at The Cloisters are made of cobblestone; and the building, a large stone fortress, has parapets around the top, arches and even a heavy metal gate at the entrance. The Cloisters holds workshops modeled on the guild system, and for six weeks "apprentices" (elementary school students) and "journeymen" (high school and college students) work with "mastercraftsmen" (teachers) to prepare for The Cloisters' Festival. They make banners to decorate the buildings, build tents and booths for the merchants and, of course, make costumes to wear to the Festival.

On Festival day they are joined by jugglers, dancers,

musicians, craftsmen demonstrating medieval arts and merchants selling authentic medieval food and wares. There is even a jousting tournament, in which two knights on horseback compete against each other. Your festival would not have to be as elaborate as The Cloisters' to be successful; decorations and costumes are the main ingredients which help create an authentic atmosphere. You can serve medieval food, such as mead, roast meat and fritters, and set up games which were played in the Middle Ages, such as chess, backgammon and blindman's buff. A medieval festival is an imaginative alternative to bake sales or street fairs, and it is a fun way to share all of the things you have learned about the Middle Ages.

CREDITS

All the works of art pictured on the following pages are from the collections of The Metropolitan Museum of Art. The particular collections and accession numbers are noted below.

Designed by Kohar Alexanian
Set in 12 pt. Trump
Composed by Royal Composing Room, Inc.
Printed by The Murray Printing Company
Bound by The Haddon Craftsmen, Inc.
HARPER & ROW, PUBLISHERS, INCORPORATED